PRAISE FOR
THE PSALMS: A SANCTUARY FOR THE SOUL

"The book of Psalms is a gift that keeps on giving. In order to receive that continuing gift, however, careful, attentive, imaginative work of interpretation is required. In this volume (and the others yet to follow), Marty Folsom does much of this hard work for us and with us. He provides playful imagery that opens vistas of communication. He offers suggestive poetry alongside the poetry of the Psalms and is steady in his focus on the God who occupies the Psalter. The reader is invited to join in this good work, to make fresh connections between this old poetry and our own lived reality."

—Walter Brueggemann, Columbia Theological Seminary

"Into the concrete jungle of 'critical and technical' Psalms commentaries, Marty Folsom brings something of an oasis-garden: For each psalm there is an accompanying interpretive paraphrase that helps draw the reader into that world through reaching out to her imagination. This and the linking comments between the treatments of the individual psalms are arresting and inviting to people seeking God's face today. It is very much in the spirit of Eugene Peterson, and by association the affective spirituality of U2's Bono, but also that of the meditative tradition of the undivided Church."

—Mark Elliott, University of St Andrews

"Wow, just wow! I love the design of this, the poetry, the invitation for people to abide in the Psalms and meditate on them. Perhaps my favorite part is the parallel of the English translation with a freer poetic version on the right. This is a beautiful way to recover the more formal translation in parallel with poetic creativity."

—Libby Backfish, Jessup University

"Already famed for his theme of reciprocity, the author has now interpreted the Psalms as taking us back into the Garden of Eden, to delight us in a wholly new perspective. Always on the margins of conventional scholarship, Dr. Folsom surprises us with this new exploration like no other scholar."

—James Houston, Regent College

The Psalms:

A Sanctuary for the Soul

Book 1: 1–30

MARTY FOLSOM

Illustrations by Abigail Folsom

Morehouse Publishing
19 East 34th Street
New York, NY 10016
www.churchpublishing.org

Morehouse Publishing is an imprint of Church Publishing Incorporated.

Cover design by Jessica Sayward Bright
Interior design by Alison Cnockaert
Illustrations by Abigail Folsom
Typeset by Westchester Publishing Services

ISBN 978-1-64065-891-2 (paperback)
ISBN 978-1-64065-892-9 (eBook)

Library of Congress Control Number: 2025950616

Dedicated to Bono,
Who, like David, sings from the heart,
Wrestles with the divine and the daily news,
And understands music as an invitation to humanity
To gather around Holy Fire.

Table of Contents

Foreword

The Psalms have been shaping the lives of Christians for two thousand years. But even when they are well translated, despite their obvious glories, they can often feel opaque and obscure, sometimes even offensive. In this remarkable book, you will find the Psalms rendered fresh, vibrant, and newly transparent to the Living God.

The literary critic George Steiner once said that the best commentary on art is more art. And that is what Marty Folsom has given us. Of course, the Psalms are Hebrew poetry; Folsom pairs each psalm with further poetry (and other media, for that matter). He invites us to listen to both together in what he calls a "stereo" reading, so that dimensions of depth in the Psalms begin to be manifest as perhaps never before.

Here we need to rid ourselves of the idea—all too common these days—that poetic verse is simply an ornamental extra, a gloss or coating, which makes the text more attractive and immediately accessible, but which can be set aside once its "message" has been grasped. This seriously underestimates the power of poetry. The medium is part of the message. God has given us a book of poetry presumably because certain dimensions of truth are accessible *only* in this way. What's more, good poetry rarely makes things instantly easier to understand. As the Russian critic Viktor Shklovsky argued, poetry typically "defamiliarizes" the world. Only when what Samuel Taylor Coleridge called "the lethargy of custom" is challenged will we be able to see the world more truthfully. Can we ever think of God the same way once we've heard him described in the Psalms as a rock or shield? Can we ever imagine the tender care of God the same way once we've been pulled into the gentle, poetic rhythm of Psalm 23? Poetry at its best reshapes our imaginations so that what we thought we knew well becomes strangely unfamiliar, and at the same time immeasurably more wonderful and compelling.

Running through every page of Folsom's book is the conviction that the Psalms are not merely objects of study, specimens for the literary analyst, but media of encounter with a God whose very heart is alive with the rhythm of love. Folsom is a serious and able teacher of the Scriptures and of the Christian tradition—there is no surrender of the intellect here, but his mental hard graft is oriented ultimately to the turning of the human heart, the rekindling of our desire for this God who loved us before we loved him. Let Folsom be your guide, and you'll likely soon find another Guide has been powerfully at work through him.

Jeremy Begbie
Duke University

Introduction

In the morning, LORD, you hear my voice;
in the morning I lay my requests before you
and wait expectantly.
(Psalm 5:3 NIV)

PROCEED WITH WONDER— ONE PSALM AT A TIME

The Psalms: A Sanctuary for the Soul walks you through each of the Psalms to experience the heart of God behind them, using the imagery or setting of a garden to deepen that connection.

God established a garden as humanity's sacred sanctuary, a place for intimate communion, experiencing profound beauty, engaging in struggles, expressing heartfelt sorrow, and ultimately discovering harmony with him. Gardens frequently appear in the Bible as symbols of engagement with God—places of reflection, renewal, and intimate connection: for example, the Garden of Gethsemane, where Jesus prayed.

Martin Luther said of the Psalms: "In them you can see into the hearts of all the saints as if you were looking at a lovely pleasure-garden, or were gazing into heaven. How fair and charming and delightful are the flowers you will find there" (Luther, Martin, quoted in Witvliet 2007, 39).

Gardens are metaphors for intimacy and vulnerability, where one can know and be known by God. This motif reflects the Psalms' themes of experiencing God's presence and pouring out one's heart to him in response. Thus, in this book, we begin with curiosity and look to the Psalms to discover that God is present and active to reveal a life worth living.

Integrating the Psalms as a spiritual practice with a garden setting, either as a physical or metaphorical space, might seem novel, but it is a natural pairing, given the Bible's frequent association of gardens with sacred encounters. God brings us to a compassionate presence—drawing us to hear his voice. In the garden of the Psalms, we find God-saturated places, creating "thin places" where heaven and earth coincide.

God loves to meet for connection, but not everything is roses. Life becomes enriched through seasons of conflict and confidence—always charged with awareness of mystery, learning to indwell the presence of God, this One who is waiting for you in this world created for connection.

The garden before you serves as the playground of discovery. So please visit regularly.

The soil of the Psalms is rich for cultivating who you are. They intend to expand your horizons and develop your giftedness for blessing others. Gardens are not objects of observation; they are auditoriums and greenhouses to make room for pruning and nurturing.

In your journey through the Psalms, you will learn to name encounters and emotions and to practice God's presence. You are never alone on this path. You will sometimes be distracted by the authentic challenges that are ever present for all humans. So much of life in this world is filled with weeds, noisy neighbors, and pests that will annoy you daily. But hearing the voice of God's heart will be our grandest goal.

Ultimately, what you have in your hands is an exercise in relational theology. What I mean by that is that all of life is about relationships, starting with the triune God, who exists in relationships and acts in the world to facilitate relationships in every aspect of our being and interactions with all of reality and each other—it's all about relationships. We will enter the text of the Bible to meet the Living God, that is, the self-revealing God who spoke, still speaks, and who desires a dynamic, interactive relationship with us. This adventure opens us to a practical encounter to know and be known by the triune God, who exists in the loving, freeing relation of Father, Son, and Holy Spirit—we are persons in relationship, initiated and sustained by the One God who made us for a life of love together. God invites us to conversation, conflict, consolation, and deepening relationships born of God's address to us.

The Psalms are not tame. They invite a life of honesty. The God of the Psalms is not beholden to the cravings of our desires. We learn to acknowledge complexities but not to fix them. We find confidence in his presence to sustain us. Welcome to the Garden of God.

CONTINUE WITH CREATIVITY AND SELECTIVITY—SAVOR EACH SECTION

This first volume will engage Psalms 1 through 30. Each chapter crafts a creative space to experience that psalm in a kaleidoscopic encounter, with a continuity of theme and a spectrum of textures.

To truly engage with a psalm, approach it like a child stepping into a realm of wonder. Prepare to use the ears and eyes of your imagination. Survey the garden space, open yourself to art, poetry, and reflection. Some of the Psalms will resonate with an ancient familiarity, grounding us in a sense of belonging. Others will unfold as a fresh, unexpected fulfillment of a long-held desire.

Just like a garden, life allows us to choose which moments to savor, capture, or bypass. Embrace the boundless grace of God's gifts. Be receptive to what resonates within your heart. You may always return to discover what you overlooked, or find that a new perspective, shaped by your own transformation, colors your renewed experience.

Some Garden Tools for Engaging the Psalms

Cultivate an awareness of God's hidden presence revealed in the Psalms and throughout your daily life. Notice the symbols guiding you to the activities, helping you understand that "You are here." Delight in the elements that resonate with you. I invite you to become a gardener, put on relational gloves and explorer's shoes, and turn on some music. Prepare for digging, admiring, planting, meandering, smelling, and enjoying what it means to indwell a blossoming space. You can pick and choose your discovery process as you enter the wonderment of the garden. Take some time to familiarize yourself with the format of each chapter using the "garden tools" discussed below.

Surveying the Garden

This survey is a brief introduction, similar to a tour guide orienting you to an art exhibition. At an opening glance, it prepares you for each psalm's message and gives you ears to hear its contribution. It is a view from the porch or the viewpoint where we can see the whole.

Into the Garden with God

As we enter each psalm, we are walking within the whole garden of the Bible. I note where other Bible verses echo the heartbeat or theme of this particular psalm. The point is to pay attention to the fact that God loves gardens as a place to meet with those in whom he delights, and to see the themes develop in other contexts. He plants themes throughout the Bible that begin to accentuate and punctuate splashes of colorful joy or pools of tearful sorrow. We are learning to identify the character of ideas within the whole Bible as presented in different locations.

The point of the Psalms is to meet and come to know the Gardener. As we wander the Psalms, we will learn to hear God's voice and know his ever-present heart. Anything that happens to you is a byproduct of this deepening plunge into his presence.

Visions of Paradise

Pictures are invitations to participate in a particular place. Each psalm will include an illustration to awaken your imagination, to help you dwell on what is going on in the text.

Think: "I am picturing myself getting ready to go into the garden."

Along the Garden Path

This section is a slow walk to hear what is happening in the psalm. This part is an exercise in attentive listening within the Garden of God. You will notice well-placed garden gates, paths, and other items of interest. These will help reveal insight from vista points where our eyes may explore more thoroughly. Emotions express our relationships to reality. Each garden walk will awaken your emotions and expand your relationships with God, others, and yourself. You will sense the path, the textures, and the world inside that is waiting to be emotionally explored. By taking time to carefully consider the emotions you might encounter within God's world, you can become more aware of the contexts shaping your life, as revealed through the journey of the Psalms. These psalms act like windows, offering glimpses into our own realities, even amidst the beauty of a garden.

Indwelling the Garden

Things get a little wilder now. We will look at the text of the psalm, not alone but set alongside a poetic rendition. Reading this section is a fluid experience, akin to listening to improvisational jazz. The traditional translation of the psalm will provide the melody. Beside it, the psalm is rewritten in rhymed poetry. Together, they create improvised harmony. I call this a stereo effect—two similar sounds in music or sights for 3D are drawn together to create depth. Thus, our stereo dynamic is created by giving you two renditions of each psalm. Let's see how that works.

When you start reading, you will see the psalm in two columns. As your eyes dance between them, you will bring together what they both point toward in your mind.

This kind of reading is an act of indwelling. What does that mean? Instead of merely looking at words on a page, for example, the word *house*, think about looking through the words to let an image of a house appear in your mind. In seeing through the words in the parallel renditions, you are indwelling them and opening your mind to hear deeply.

Hearing more deeply for hidden emotions, look at the words I *love you*. You might see these words as a combination of black marks on the paper. But think about listening *through* the words to *hear* the speaker's heart and *intent*. In that way, you are indwelling the emotions of the words. You are becoming attentive, indwelling the other person's poetic intentions.

Here is a practice text. Try reading both columns simultaneously, creating the stereo effect. On the left is the English-language translation. The right is a poetic rendition in *italics*.

The LORD is my shepherd, I shall not want.

Confidence supreme in meadow green,
I live within Your care,
Lacking nothing I may need,
You shepherd me full aware.

Taking Reflections with You

This section helps you reflect on what you have experienced. It is designed to capture snapshots of what stood out to you.

It is vital for you to relax and gather insights to gain an awareness of God's presence. In reflection, you may experience interrelatedness between you and God and maybe with others. Let the thoughts weave in and out to interlace your hearts together.

This practice employs a modified and expanded form of *Lectio Divina*, which means a "divine reading." A *Lectio Divina* reflection allows you to listen more deeply. To assist you in your reflections, we will provide questions to explore what you have read and actions that now stand open to you. For example:

- First, *Lectio, reading the words*—What words or ideas stood out for you in this psalm?
- Second, *Meditatio, meditation*—What does this psalm say about God?
- Third, *Oratio, speaking to you*—What does the psalm say about you?
- Fourth, *Contemplatio, contemplation, embracing the relationship*—What does this psalm say about your relationship with God?
- Fifth, *Intuitive listening*—I add this as an invitation to hear God speak to you from what you have just read—Can you listen for what God is saying directly to you?
- Finally, *Informal response*—Articulate what comes to mind as your personal response to God in a dialogue with what you have just read. What do you want to say in return?

Final Embrace

As you exit each psalm, one final free-form poem captures the garden psalm's emotion as an embrace that deeply resonates with your soul.

I strongly encourage you to read these out loud. These scripts bear the imprint of the soul, learning to find a new language that needs to be spoken to really be heard.

Also, read them as slowly as possible. This is a simmering time for the heart. As you read unhurriedly, your meditation becomes an entry to indwell the words, felt as your own. They become a sanctuary for processing what your soul is discovering.

Think of this section as a closing prayer. It is a reflection and an invitation to take heart, echoes, and enriched visions of intimacy with you from the garden. Take it as a moment to savor the presence of God as you go on your journey.

Psalm 1

Pathfinding

Blessed is the one . . . whose delight is in the law of the LORD*,*
and who meditates on his law day and night.
(Psalm 1:1–2 NIV)

Surveying the Garden

In the midst of all times and places, you have chosen this moment to stand where Jesus stood, at the entrance to the Psalms. He stood here as a human entering into a dialogue with his Father while wrestling with being human. You, too, are invited to meet with the Living God. Jesus still goes with us on this journey as he promised to be always with us. This first psalm guides your journey through the garden and life. You may have gotten out of bed, and in that haze, you are unsure where you are going or what is most important in your life. This psalm encourages reorientation, guiding you to walk wisely with God. Don't forget: You are standing at the Welcoming Gate.

The question for you today is: "Who will you listen to in order to be fully alive?" The answer will shape your life and who you will be. Each day's choices and opportunities shape who you will become in your relationships with God and others, and how you spend your time.

Calm your spirit and listen intently as you approach the psalm, allowing yourself to truly hear its message.

Hear him say, "I am ready to walk with you. Are you open to this adventure?"

What is your response?

Into the Garden with God

Today, you are at a crossroads. But it's unlike any other crossroads you have encountered. God has spoken for a long time to those who stand at crossroads. Yesterday had crossroads, tomorrow will too. Every decision, no matter how small, began at a crossroads, shaping your path and influencing your relationships, even if only slightly. Every act, from getting out of bed, caring for yourself, and serving others to investing in changing the world, impacts you in your relationship with others.

Today, you are at a specific intersection as you journey into the Psalms. You are here, embarking on a path of discovery.

God gives us paths in life; you could have chosen many other routes. Today, the most powerful catalyst for your awakening and growth isn't the path itself, but who you choose to walk it with.

On this day, on this adventure, what matters is that you go with the Creator God, who knows and loves you. When the people of Israel stood ready to enter the Promised Land, they had to make a choice. In that respect, you stand with them today, and God speaks to you along with them, saying:

> **"I call heaven and earth to witness against you today, that I have placed before you life and death, the blessing and the curse. So choose life in order that you may live, you and your descendants, [20] by loving the LORD your God, by obeying His voice, and by holding close to Him."**
>
> (Deuteronomy 30:19–20 NASB)

Hear his invitation, not as a command, but as the call to come home. He is waiting for you in the garden. The gate is unlocked.

Visions of Paradise

Along the Garden Path

As we enter, think about your attitude. It takes courage to step forward, let go, and say to yourself, "I am open and ready."

Entering the Psalms, we are stepping into a world apart from our ordinary lives. It is like going through the Looking Glass with Alice, but in this case, it's a journey *from* a mad world *into* a world where the madness is embraced and healed. Here, we find a lifescape where every facet of human existence is freely and unconditionally held.

In our ordinary world, we are guided by laws, individual rights, material pursuits, the quest for self-determination, and all manner of self-improvement coaches—all reinforced by following established rules. In the Psalms, *Law* refers to the Torah. For the Jews (and us), this points to the revelation of God to Moses. God calls for a response. The Law is *not* a set of constraints or legislation; it is a story of unconditional love, unreservedly given. However, there are consequences for walking away: one can get lost.

The Torah is the story of God's covenant with a chosen people entrusted with spreading that blessing to others. It evokes feelings by engaging the mind and the past. This text invites us to walk together and meditate on its persistent whisper, "I have brought you to myself; now live out of that love."

This attitude exemplifies how Jesus entered this psalm and began his ministry, deepening his relationship with his Father (Abba) and dedicating himself to his people.

You are entering a realm of covenant relationships that will test you in your relationships with your neighbors and God. Our relationship with God will only function with a radical, open honesty. Hiding will result in lying, building protective walls, and donning deceptive masks. To embrace a life of deeper connection, one must remain open to learning from God and those we cherish.

You are entering a place with the final promise of shalom. True peace is the fruit of togetherness, even though challenges are inevitable. Here, we find peace in relation to God and our neighbor. Embrace all that surrounds you, even as conflicts and complaints persist in your head. Find contentment and connection as you move forward.

As you enter this place, feel the presence of God by your side, embracing you.

Indwelling the Garden

Get ready to put on your headphones.

Stereo is achieved for you by aligning the two perspectives and seeing them simultaneously to create depth. This effect is always the case with both sight and sound, which is why we have two ears and eyes to apprehend the depth of what surrounds us. Focus on living in the unifying experience to enter fully into it.

Glance back and forth as you read. See what is created in your mind and spirit.

[1] How blessed is the man who
does not walk in the counsel of
the wicked,
Nor stand in the path of sinners,
Nor sit in the seat of scoffers!

Sitting snug in Your embrace,
The arms that bid me walk in
grace,
No longer pulled by gripping lies,
That life of fear that blurs the eyes.

2 But his delight is in the law of the
LORD,
And in His law he meditates day
and night.

Delight shall be my beacon guide,
The Spirit's word blooms from inside,
My mind shall rest in hearing true,
From dawn to dusk, I'll walk with You.

3 He will be like a tree *firmly*
planted by streams of water,
Which yields its fruit in its season,
And its leaf does not wither;
And in whatever he does, he
prospers.

This jostling journey's just begun,
I've found my home-root in
the One
Who grows me like the ripening crop,
Abundant yield when the harvest's
brought.

4 The wicked are not so,
But they are like chaff which the
wind drives away.

Gone, oh glad, the days of spoil,
That life spilled out like olive oil,
The waste of promise left to decay
Till days unsavored were whisked away.

5 Therefore the wicked will not
stand in the judgment,
Nor sinners in the assembly of the
righteous.

Missed, the days that might have been,
Leaving memories buried within.
Frivolity's fruit is a useless toil,
A depleted soul with self-pleasure's
spoil.

6 For the LORD knows the way of
the righteous,
But the way of the wicked will
perish.

Remind me again, oh King of Days,
To feast on the love that shapes our ways.
It is ever tragic to miss Your delight,
To wander in darkness and miss the light.

Reflect for a moment on the experience created as you glanced down this psalm as a path. Prepare to be open to what is possible after reading this psalm. Where did it leave you?

Taking Reflections with You

To help soak in the invitation of Psalm 1, we will consider the effect of this psalm on our relationships. The following exercise aims to rearrange your relational life to move toward intimacy with God and others.

This reflection will take time to answer, so savor the discovery process. Let thoughts develop into stories of relating as you encounter each question below. Each inquiry will focus on a different aspect of the relations implied in the psalm to make the reflections more explicit. This exercise is a process of learning to pay rapt attention.

- First, what words jumped out at you from this psalm? Take a moment to look back. Maybe circle a few words or phrases or jot them down. What images come to you with those words?
- Next, explore what this psalm says *about* God. What words from either column reveal something about God's attitude to you? Do you feel his presence or absence as you move through it? What insights help you go forward in knowing him as One wanting to be known? Do you feel known and loved?
- Now, inquire about what the psalm says *about you*. How did you feel as you read? Did you resonate with the words, or were they foreign and vague? What desires did it awaken in you? If the psalm were a mirror for reflection on yourself, what would you wish you were more of and what less of? Did you like who you were as you exited the reading?
- What does this psalm say about *your relationship with God*? What words describe the dynamic of being with one another, depicting how you care for each other? Do you wish for something more or different than what currently exists? What phrase captures the nature of your relationship right now?
- Now stop and ask what the LORD is saying to you. This kind of listening is an act of reflection. Let what has been told from the psalm speak to you. The Spirit of God is sent to bring God's living voice to your thoughts. It might begin, "I am ready to embrace you . . . ," taken from the first line of my poetic rendition of Psalm 1:1. Listening in reflection is a key skill to learn.
- What do you want to reply? You might say, "I am ready to walk with someone who loves me . . ." Any response is the beginning of prayer as dialogue.

Let the words roll around in your mind like a new fruit or dessert you have never tasted. The voice in your head is your relational response. You may ask, "What voice in my head?" It is the very voice asking, "What voice in my head?" Our task is to let this voice of meditation speak from hearing the voice of Jesus by the Spirit. Learning to listen matters in life and love—it is the path to the connection that Psalm 1 opens.

Final Embrace

This final exercise is like a closing prayer. Read each one slowly and out loud. Take enough time to let the thoughts resonate in you. This poem is a free-form rendering of the psalm to hear the emotions that flow through the psalm. Let it draw out your emotions, which are your relationship to what you encounter. Listen for your heart to say yes to some phrases and no to others. Sweet smells are the yes that invites you to lean in and breathe deep. Things you want to prune away are the no in your spirit.

Paths.
Choices and voices.
Listening and longing.
Wanting and waiting.
Wanting the hum of You.
Resonating with Your fullness.
Washing out regret.
The clean, the smell of hope.
Embraced.
Wanted.
Willing and weak.
To wallow or waltz.
I glance ahead.
I disrobe the past.
I am healed at Your feast.
Your hand.
My heart.
One step.
Not to follow.
Not to lead.
Only going.
With.
You.

Breathe deep as you step out into your life of pathfinding.

Psalm 2

Embraced in the Storm

I will proclaim the Lord*'s decree:*
He said to me, "You are my son; today I have become your father."
(Psalm 2:7 NIV)

Surveying the Garden

Life is not always easy.

Troubling times come, and you may feel small. Troublemakers dominate your emotional horizon. The prophets of the Old Testament felt this. The Israelites felt this and may still. Jesus lived in this state as well. Today, you are not alone in feeling small and vulnerable. You don't need to turn a blind eye to this reality.

Psalm 2 prepares you to face the challenges of each new day. Also, it helps you find a steadying place of belonging with God. Disturbing situations invade your dreams, your waking moments, or segments of your day. You are not alone. Distractions prevent you from connecting with others. But this psalm invites you to know the God who will always stand with you.

The challenge for you is to center yourself in God's majesty, despite the efforts of those who try to intimidate you because they do not think like you or affirm you. Right now, it is the Creator of the universe and One who cares about you.

Say to yourself, "I am not alone."

This is a moment when you align with reality. You are entering into a personal reality with someone who cares about you. His name is Jesus, which means, "I will save you." He's up to something big.

Focus on him. As you approach the psalm, be aware of the noises around you. They will not go away. But if you let the Spirit help you hear the Son who speaks, these irritants will become like gusts of wind.

Hear him say, "I am yours, and you are mine." What is your response?

Into the Garden with God

Today you shelter in the garden. God does not remove those who bully, oppress, or make us feel small or worthless. But God provides a sanctuary of peace amid a world consumed by manipulation, selfishness, abuse, and blind ambition. You are permitted to choose who you will be in the face of this situation.

Today, you will become aware that those who plot against God are pervasive in this world. God is not disturbed. He laughs at their efforts at empire building. He lets them play their little games. In contrast, God's voice speaks and reaches out to the oppressed every day.

God leads us on our path in life. As we saw with Psalm 1, there are other trajectories that we could have chosen. To feel alive, it is not about the path we choose but who we go with that matters most.

During troubling times and facing callous indifference from the crowds and even his disciples, Jesus sought his Father in prayer. He maintained a calm, restful focus to find peace amidst many challenges:

> "Come to me, all who are weary and burdened, and I will give you rest. [29] Take my yoke upon you and learn from me, for I am gentle and humble in heart, and YOU WILL FIND REST FOR YOUR SOULS."
> (Matthew 11:28–29 NASB)

Today, hear him speaking words that show he knows your situation. Also, know that he has created a refuge for you here in the garden within his welcome. He has a hammock waiting for you to slip into like a restful embrace.

Visions of Paradise

Along the Garden Path

What is stopping you?

How does fear limit you in your love of God, your neighbor, and yourself?

How do you feel when approaching a place thick with tension? Who would you want to go with to keep you safe in this space?

Can you let yourself say, "I am afraid, but I am also ready to release the fear and be embraced by the Servant King"?

Entering this psalm, you may become profoundly aware of our ordinary world and its disarray. There might not be kings today as there were when this psalm was written, but there are bosses, politicians, and others in authority who will impact your life and cause you anxiety. Humans knock us off balance daily, whether intruding, resisting us, or just being contrary to our values. They disturb us and unravel the web of trust in our relationships.

This psalm creates a holy place, meaning a place "set aside for connection."

A friend who was studying Judaism once told me she had found a writing that said:

> **At the center of the world is Israel.**
>
> **At the center of Israel is Jerusalem.**
>
> **At the center of Jerusalem is the Temple.**
>
> **At the center of the Temple is the Holy of Holies.**
>
> **At the center of the Holy of Holies is the Ark of the covenant.**
>
> **And beneath the ark is a stone, and that is the cornerstone.**

That cornerstone is a holy person who is appointed to facilitate connection. He is enthroned in this psalm as the world's ruler. He is set aside to connect God and humanity and usher in the kingdom of God—a peaceable kingdom. He is a beloved son, an identification used here of King David and later of the Son, Jesus.

As you enter this psalm, you find yourself standing in his Holy Throne Room, the meeting place of God and humanity. Today, you will see the Father's Holy One, anointed as the Messiah, God's Son revealed. He is the hope for God's future, the cornerstone upon which his story is built.

Still yourself and absorb the wonder of this place and Person. Recognize that it is set apart from the clamor of the world. Hear the roar behind you and the calm in front of you as you adore this One and unexpectedly find yourself embraced and adored as his beloved.

You are the living epitome of human experience, standing before a holy God. You are without fear. This God stands *against* destruction and *for* those who need restoration. You may sense his resistance against those who conspire against him. He stops conspiracies that lead to violence and brings his peace. The schemers seek liberation *from* God's authority, but he brings true freedom *as* God.

There is a bigger story here. One day, God will gather all nations to this, his Holy Mountain. At present, we see world powers locked in conflict. They will rise and fall. This psalm declares that this place and this person will persist. As U2 sings, "kingdoms rise and kingdoms fall, but you go on and on" (U2, "October," *October*).

With each psalm, we will spend time in a part of the Garden of God. Today, imagine a holy hill in the garden's center. From it, you can see all that surrounds it. This is the view of the kingdom of God on earth; from his vantage point, he sees and sustains all he made. The kingdom is not distant—it is immanent, present as he accompanies his creation.

If you imagine yourself with him at the top, you may begin to feel the boundless nature of God—he rules the universe. You will be with someone as humble as a backyard farmer and wiser than any human king or ruler. You may want to burst out into song, unleash a song of joy, with delight welling up inside you and spilling over. You may notice that the birds and trees are already joining in.

This is a sheltered landscape that is safe and secure. In the distance, you can hear the defiant sound of human progress—the unbridled conflict of wills, fighting for control.

But above it all comes God's laughter at the petty games humans play. The leaders have lost touch with loving God's freedom, living in the sandbox of self-importance like self-centered children.

The musical laughter of God is soothing. It disarms those on the outside. Who could have known that his laughter could rearrange our perspective on everything?

To our surprise, the clamor and bustle of the cityscape is never muffled. God has made them integral to this place's meaningfulness. The Gardener works like a Grand Musician. He translates the contradiction and confusion outside into a symphony, rejuvenating the world he loves to fulfill his purposes. This stirs our hearts, and we join the chorus.

Feel the tension released as he embraces you. He is ready to walk by your side as you enter this place.

Indwelling the Garden

Are your headphones ready?

Hear the contesting voices within this psalm—the nations in one ear and God in the other, each speaking distinctly, yet audible together within this moment. The Creator God rules the world with mercy and compassion and speaks to set all aright. His voice, converging with the world, simultaneously brings the sound of clashing and celebration.

Remember to glance back and forth as you read.

The nations are conspiring. The Father is honoring his Son. The Son is clad as King. The Spirit calls the nations to revere this worthy One. And you—breathe with astonishment!

Hear the voices, but do not be discouraged; let your heart be drawn to wonder.

1 Why are the nations in an
uproar,
And the peoples devising a vain
thing?

Distracted by the daily grind,
Complaining wildly, voices pined.
People seek the fleeting things,
When lost, an empty echo rings.

2 The kings of the earth take their
stand,
And the rulers take counsel
together
Against the LORD and against His
Anointed, saying:

Leaders walk a lonely road,
Resolute to bear their load.
Neglecting help found right at
hand
From King and Son who rule the land.

3 "Let us tear their fetters apart
And cast away their cords from us!"

Boasts their arrogance loud and strong,
"To no one else will we belong."
Their urge for freedom is a trap,
Rebellion braids a prison strap.

4 He who sits in the heavens
laughs,
The LORD scoffs at them.

Almighty Maker of the earth,
Laughs at this struggle begun at birth,
Thinking one can run away
From strongest love to build with clay.

5 Then He will speak to them in
His anger
And terrify them in His fury,
saying,

Resounds the voice to clear the head,
To wake their senses from the dead,
"My love insists the building way,
I stand against your self-decay."

6 "But as for Me, I have installed
My King
Upon Zion, My holy mountain."

"Today, a royal head is crowned,
His loyalty to Me—renowned.
From My mountain, He shall care,
Restoring wholeness everywhere."

7 "I will surely tell of the decree of
the LORD:
He said to Me, 'You are My Son,
Today I have begotten You.

Announce the goodness of the King,
Who brings His heart to change all
things.
His Son, beloved, stands affirmed,
Birthed to regal task confirmed.

8 'Ask of Me, and I will surely give
the nations as Your inheritance,
And the *very* ends of the earth as
Your possession.

Gifting all the earth to Him,
Including all that fly or swim,
From east to west shall be His keep,
As you rise and while you sleep.

9 'You shall break them with a rod
of iron,
You shall shatter them like
earthenware.'"

10 Now therefore, O kings, show
discernment;
Take warning, O judges of the
earth.

11 Worship the LORD with
reverence,
And rejoice with trembling.

12 Do homage to the Son, that He
not become angry, and you
perish in the way,
For His wrath may soon be
kindled.
How blessed are all who take
refuge in Him!

The iron shackles He shall break,
All bent to destruction, He will shake.
Breaking up old pots of clay,
Preparing to plant another day.

Take heed, all you who lead the way,
Live from reverence; start today!
Find the wise way from those lips,
Who spoke the mountains and valley
dips.

Burst your heart in full-sung song
To Him who spans the ages long,
Let tender joy flow through your
limbs,
Amazed to pleasure in front of Him.

Kiss the Son and feel his glory
Embrace His jealous, loving story.
Find your "safe" in Sonship's arms
Blessed to live, freed from harm.

Think about the times when you felt the world was against you. Then think of those who came to your side to give you hope. Let this psalm teach you to sense the safety in the garden, even while aware of the threats outside. Rest in this moment and the hope of this place.

Let your soul be calmed with lingering attentiveness. The King's embrace beckons you from His throne to be with him.

Taking Reflections with You

To help you soak in Psalm 2, consider how it invites you to move toward intimacy with the King of Glory and be calmed from the storms that come in your daily challenges.

Let each inquiry below direct you to the relations revealed in this psalm. Swish them around in your brain to sense flashes of awareness of the challenges and the comfort.

- What images jumped out at you from the phrases in this psalm? Try glancing back. Maybe circle a few words or phrases or jot them down. What images do those *words* awaken in you?
- Explore what this psalm says *about* God. What opens up as you come before him and sense his majesty? What is new in how you see God overseeing the earth, including all those leaders and nations trying to challenge God's rule?
- What does Psalm 2 say *about you*? Did you identify with those who try to break God's influence in your life, or were you comforted that he stands against those who crave power in this world? What feelings did you have seeing the Messiah anointed as King and the impact on your life in that he is a servant King?
- What does this psalm say about *your relationship with* God? What words describe the dynamic of your being a child of the King? Do you feel that you care for this One who cares for you? What would change if you could playfully laugh out loud because you are with the King, who is deeply fond of you?
- What is the LORD *saying* to you through this psalm? Reflect and let the Spirit whisper the living voice of God to your mind out of your meditation. Yes, read again and let the Spirit echo into your spirit—"I am here to help you. Find your 'safe' as you rest in my arms, blessed to live and freed from what seeks to harm you."
- What do you want to *answer*? Continue with prayer as dialogue.

Allow yourself to settle into the thoughts that draw you to trust this One who loves you.

In your mind, shrink the people and situations that bedevil you to the size of toy soldiers. Minimize them, remove their threat, and make some space for sanity.

In light of this psalm, hear the voice of the Spirit announce in this Throne Room, "This is the Father's beloved Son." Sit in the presence of the Enthroned King who encircles your life with compassion, even as he enfolds the globe. Here, heaven and earth are united in him, and his divine reign restores the land.

Final Embrace

This closing prayer of reflection is also an invitation to let your emotions attune to being embraced. Let the words discover something in you as you speak them.

Come back often when things are tough; reenter this space for reorientation. You may find that it speaks to you differently each time you return.

Adoration.
Shedding fearful malformation.
Needing love's alteration.
Undone.
Wanting Your transformation.
Yet.
So loud, so pushed.
Weak against the pressing.
So much needs redressing.
A Glance.
A Hope.
A hill where love elopes.
Breaking all the rules.
Ruled by love alone.
Could this be home?
Memories call me back.
All I see is lack.
Yet a holy moment comes.
Awake.
I see what is at stake.
The bliss.
The Kiss.
The King who calls my name.
Blessed.

Psalm 3

Rhythms of Restoration

I lie down and sleep; I wake again, because the Lord *sustains me.*
I will not fear though tens of thousands assail me on every side.
(Psalm 3:5–6 NIV)

Surveying the Garden

Welcome to a moment of rest in God's garden.

Do you need rest?

Do you wish the day were just beginning or wish you were at the end?

Psalms 3 and 4 serve as bookends: one welcomes the morning, while the other concludes the day.

Psalm 3 invites you to deeply feel your past disappointments, current challenges, or coming dangers. It takes seriously those things that disturb your sleep, drain you, or overwhelm you, still lingering in the morning.

The psalm intends to lift your chin as you come face-to-face with the Living God. You may need renewal just as much as King David, the author. He was a man after God's own heart—and also very human and vulnerable.

This psalm is for the morning after a hard day. It permits you to cry out in honesty about your situation.

Rather than reliving the struggle once more, the psalm asks you to be honest and say what you feel. Anger, frustration, defeat, depression, and more are possible here. Scan your emotions as you recall yesterday.

He says, "I am here to listen."

Try responding, "Oh God, I feel so ______ today; this is where I am."

You may often feel abandoned or provoked, gripped by intense moods, or experience emptiness. Let yourself feel this morning's cool in the garden—know you are not alone. As you exhale your honest emotions, breathe in the acceptance awakened by God's presence.

The Accompanying God is here to protect you, sustain you, and help you ride out the churning and the aching inside.

God's name is I AM. He says, "I *Am* with you to push through the riptides of discontent that arise from life's breakdowns. Hold on to me."

Selah, a Hebrew term you will encounter in this psalm, means rest or pause. It invites you to stop and rest your mind and body. Give yourself a moment to experience God's presence as he restores you to a place of peace and well-being, to a feeling of being loved.

Hear him say, "Let Me hold you; that was a tough night; rest in My embrace." Can you relax by refocusing on being held?

Into the Garden with God

The recovery process begins as soon as you accept that you are upset. Blurt it out like David!

Acknowledge your displeasure, then let Jesus's presence reveal a deeper reality that will change your heart. He is the constant on your daily roller coaster, a steady presence amidst the unpredictable.

Let your insecurity and feeling of being out of control move you towards confidence in God. We cannot change our situations, but we can change our relationship with them. Handing over your issues to someone you trust opens you up to unexpected and unrealized outcomes. This "change of mind" represents the transformative moment occurring throughout the Psalms.

In the Garden of Gethsemane, Jesus had to be honest about what transpired as tensions mounted. He disappointed those who wanted him to be more decisive in advancing their agendas. Amidst the pressures, he was able to be honest about his desperation. In the end, he could let it go. He was where you have been or still are, crying out for another way.

Jesus prayed to his Abba. Amidst troubling times, he learned to let go and trust that he would be sustained into the future. Today, you are invited to find solace in the garden with One who has faced adversity and come out victorious. Realign with God's restorative justice as you experience the feeling of release. This happened for Jesus:

> And He went a little beyond *them*, and fell to the ground and *began* praying that if it were possible, the hour might pass Him by. [36] And He was saying, "Abba! Father! All things are possible for You; remove this cup from Me; yet not what I will, but what You *will*."
> (Mark 14:35–36 NASB)

If you are not feeling tense today, try telling yourself, "My life is perfect." See if a voice comes back into your thinking to give you some exceptions. They sound like: "It is pretty good, except . . ." Let those exceptions be your stepping stones to discovery. Take one step of honesty as you learn to acknowledge and release. Journey into the labyrinth of exploration, its path leading you to meet God at its center. Then try releasing as you wander out.

Visions of Paradise

This is a healing labyrinth. Consider walking it to leave behind your mental pollution. Find rest in the center with God. You may come out fresh when leaving the emotional residue with God in the center.

Along the Garden Path

Stop at the start of this psalm. Feel the exhaustion and stresses that may swirl in or around you. Look them in the face and say, "I see you there."

This psalm uses battle imagery, pictures of shields and victory. What is the form of your battlefield? Is it at work, at home, in a relationship, or with your finances?

Bring the stories of your battle with you so that you can be specific about the trauma you've experienced. Although we do not often acknowledge the hidden pains, they are the genuine stress felt in your shoulders and neck. They may manifest as a headache or a groan you feel escaping when you think about what weighs on you.

This psalm opens a place of protection. Wherever your heart may be as you enter, spend time in this psalm to let it move you to moments of *peace*. It is not just about pausing from battle, it's *about allowing* your heart to find rest *in him*.

Feel him by your side as you enter this psalm.

Indwelling the Garden

Remember to hear with stereo listening as you enter the psalm.

Savor the words as you read so you feel them in your body. See what is created in your mind and spirit. Pause and let the selah moments sink in.

1 O Lord, how my enemies have
increased!
Many are rising up against me.

Standing here before the tide
Of shoving people full of pride,
The daily turn of push and pull,
My patience spent, frustration full.

2 Many are saying of my soul,
"There is no salvation for him in
God."
[Selah]

Hateful shouts do pierce my heart,
Wearing thin my strength to start
Another day with pressing cries,
"Your helpful God is full of lies."
[I rest in You]

3 But You, LORD, are a shield around me,
My glory, and the One who lifts my head.

Still yearns my soul to calm in You,
Find solace in Your arms so true.
You bright my way and dim my fears,
You lift my chin and kiss my tears.

4 I was crying to the LORD with my voice,
And He answered me from His holy mountain. [Selah]

My mournful sobbing in the night,
So burdened by my daily plight,
You heard, and gentle word replied,
Majestic whisper by my side.
[I rest in You]

5 I lay down and slept;
I awoke, for the LORD sustains me.

Healing sleep, how sweet the night,
I rest my head in Your delight.
Refreshed again with waking dew,
You bid me rise and walk with You.

6 I will not be afraid of ten thousands of people
Who have set themselves against me all around.

Fear will flee when light appears,
Shadows dash when brilliance cheers,
Encroaching foes, I will not fear,
My heart still knows that You are near.

7 Arise, LORD; save me, my God!
For You have struck all my enemies on the cheek;
You have shattered the teeth of the wicked.

Arise, my King, who holds my all,
Keep me from destruction's fall,
You have been my sure defense,
Your protection builds my confidence.

8 Salvation belongs to the LORD;
May Your blessing be upon Your people!
[Selah]

Renewal comes from God our King,
From loss to life, He makes to sing,
His joy wells up to breathe within,
His peace surrounds and holds us in.
[I rest in You]

Pause for a moment of peace. Rest your mind in the thought that loving arms surround you. Let the joy begin to rise up in the calm that opens. Feel the cleansing. Accept the love that knows your name.

Taking Reflections with You

Psalm 3 accepts that we have complicated relationships, but they do not need to overwhelm us.

Its words hope to rearrange your relation to the rigors of life. Finding confidence begins with seeking honest expressions. Then, we are prepared for life as space is created for enriching relationships.

Reflect on the psalm, pay attention to its words, and listen to your responses.

- What images touched you in this psalm? Highlight specific words or phrases with colors to draw out emotional responses. What is revealed about your life in those words?
- Next, explore what this psalm says *about* God. Where is God for you as you read the psalm? Can you feel his presence or absence as you move through the psalm? What is missing for you, and what is clarified in knowing his part in your story as you read?
- Now, look at what the psalm says *about you*. Did you feel honest with yourself and God? What unresolved issues did it awaken in you? Did you notice any restoration as you exited the reading? When did you last feel restored and whole? Who were you trying to be in that story?
- Finally, ask what this psalm says about *your relationship with God*. Did you feel you could describe your relation to God with no holds barred as you went along? Can you imagine a daily practice of honestly pouring out what churns in you as you meet with God? Having read and thought about the words, what one phrase captures the nature of your relationship with God right now?
- Listen for Jesus's voice. What are you hearing *the* LORD say to you as an echo of the psalm? Let the living voice of God calm

your mind and speak, if you need that, or affirm your honesty as you authentically empty out your emotions.

- What do you want to *say back*? Continue with prayer, being grateful, curious, or looking for a next step to connection! This dialogue is the path of learning relational interaction that draws us together.

Listen to the emotional compass in you that points to the problems that need addressing. The needle may point to unmet expectations that could be let go.

Consider that salvation is a form of mental health. It is a focused form of spiritual health that feels like intimacy—knowing and being known just as we are. This honest closeness is our goal. It involves shedding the resistance that makes you raw inside with disappointment or anger. Further, it means accepting the salve of God's healing brilliance, like pulling back the curtains and letting the light into a dark room.

Final Embrace

You are invited to come back and enter this space again. You may find that you experience it differently each time you return. Follow the flow of these words to wash out your emotionally clogged days.

Startled.
Anger rents my room.
My thoughts are consumed.
Resistance.
Persistence.
Feeling silenced.
Defenseless.
Distrustful.
Life is such a handful.
Thrashing in the night.
Why this empty fight?
That whisper.
That word.
No, it's the Voice.
Giving me a choice.
Spilling, spewing—
Or a breath of renewing.
Those leeches can become speechless.
My ears renew to hear You.
The only place to be true.
The meeting tent goes up.
Fragile.
The stakes dug deep.
Sheltered.
You're here.
Shielded.
Surrounded.
Safe.
Secure.

Psalm 4

Resting in Light of Reality

Many, LORD, are asking, "Who will bring
us prosperity?"
Let the light of your face shine on us.
Fill my heart with joy when their grain and new
wine abound.
(Psalm 4:6–7 NIV)

Surveying the Garden

Another day is done.

Not all evenings are filled with sunsets. Some days end with beauty. But sometimes . . .

Some days end with you collapsing on the floor, soaked from the downpour of rain or the weight of voices that left you exhausted. This psalm is for relief from that kind of day.

Psalm 4 invites you to feel the weight of a drenching day and the sheltering presence of the night. You may still be shaken by corrosive chatter that lingers in your head. Listen now for the calming voice of the One who calls you beloved.

This psalm is a pavilion for peace. It invites you to a place of personal connection, where your heart is lifted and your nerves calmed. Experience a unique serenity that can only flourish in the company of being with the One you trust without question.

Come, find a place to sleep in the garden as one watched over.

Hear Jesus say, "That was a day to lay aside. Come now, and rest in My presence. Allow yourself to drift into joyful dreams." Respond with the request: "May I unwind in the embrace of your peace?" Slip into his outstretched arms.

Into the Garden with God

The Bible frequently portrays peaceful rest as a desirable state.

God's voice brings a profound calm to address the inner turmoil in our heads and hearts.

Don't try to listen for a voice from heaven to suddenly shout out.

Listen to his voice in your head saying, "I am here." Yes, use your imagination to engage with reality. He remains present, though unseen, and only his sheep truly recognize the sound of his voice.

Reflect on the name Immanuel, which means "God with us," and let this thought create a sense of his presence. This opening allows the light of his face to shine on you. Sit with that.

Then, let's explore a practical way to cultivate our listening skills. We are going to take a verse that talks about God and change the pronouns. So where it would say "the Lord," we will put "I." Then, it is coming from his mouth, directed to you. This shift works anywhere in the Psalms. For example, hear Psalm 4:8 from Jesus, "I will make you lie down and sleep in peace, I am your LORD and I will make you dwell in My safety."

With realignment comes the promise of serious dialogue and deep connection. Discovery and dialogue are made possible by listening instead of talking about another person. Can you feel the difference between *talking about* someone silently sitting next to you and *listening* to them in order to learn about them? Only one of these modes is effective in creating a meaningful personal connection.

The blessing of Aaron from Numbers 6:24–26 is an example. It is a beautiful blessing, but as you sit in this garden with Jesus, it is an even more powerful affirmation.

Receive this blessing, a gift of peace given by God that transcends ordinary human understanding. Feel this blessing blanket you as you rest in him. The original begins, "The LORD bless you. . . ." We will change the pronouns and listen to him speak to us.

24 *I* will bless you, and keep you;
25 *I* will make My face shine on you, and be gracious to you;
26 *I* will turn My face toward you and give you peace.
(NASB)

Do you feel resistance inside, or can you accept his voice? It is easiest to recognize that your mental life, your memories, and your dreams involve using your imagination. Jesus comes now as the Word that speaks, and we are using this creative listening skill to envision the light of his face as he leads you to a place where you will enjoy the most renewing sleep of your life.

Visions of Paradise

This pavilion of peace invites restoration from the day's challenges, and you can feel the renewal in this place dedicated to a secure sleep.

Along the Garden Path

This psalm establishes a stark contrast. On the one hand, we are burdened by delusive echoes from the past. We have come across similar troublemakers on our previous walks in the Psalms, the kind of tricksters who thrive on empty promises and fabricated delusions. They are seductive; they promise prosperity, but they perplex us. Their promises will never bring peace. We bear bruises from their impact on our lives.

On the other hand, we look forward to dwelling in the Living God's care. This psalm invites us to sit with the One who sees our hearts. He wants to heal us from the injuries of the past so we can sustain ourselves in his future.

Imagine the sounds of joyful flutes filling the air with soulful music. They bring a fresh, gentle wind that will carry your heart skyward.

In the distance, we also hear drums. They will attempt to shatter our peace. Let the flutes lift you; relax, and feel yourself drift into the evening light.

That light is coming from the face of the One beside you. Let the light and the music settle you. Let the psalm take you from tension to release, where all the static and noise can be lost in the calming instant of this moment.

Your ears and heart are now attuning to Jesus's presence. Soak in restful joy as a companion of the Caretaker of Souls. He is the host who makes room for weary travelers like you.

Indwelling the Garden

As the shadows lengthen and the curtain of night falls, attune your heart and eyes to enter the calm of this psalm.

1 Answer me when I call, O God
of my righteousness!
You have relieved me in my
distress;
Be gracious to me and hear my
prayer.

Waiting again to hear Your voice,
You, in whom my prayers rejoice.
Make room for me to dwell in bliss,
To know Your presence as a kiss.

2 O sons of men, how long will
my honor become a reproach?
How long will you love what
is worthless and aim at
deception? [Selah]

Wanderer, how long will your eyes divert,
When, from that stare, will you revert?
Has lust for smoke doused your love for
the fire?
Grasping at shadow-shapes, you fall on
a pyre.
[I rest in You]

3 But know that the LORD has
set apart the godly man for
Himself;
The LORD hears when I call to
Him.

Sweet firstfruit, the Vinedresser tenderly
saves,
A humble person whose passion is brave.
His listening ear attends to my needs,
So, I wholeheartedly follow wherever
He leads.

4 Tremble, and do not sin;
Meditate in your heart upon
your bed, and be still. [Selah]

A reverent shout now bursts from my soul,
Shedding illusions of my self-control.
Let my heart bathe again in the stillness
of You,
Breathe colors in me to change my life's
hue.
[I rest in You]

[5] Offer the sacrifices of
righteousness,
And trust in the LORD.

My heart-gift I offer with thanks sprung anew,
Abandon my worries to nest in Your true.
Your faithfulness near sustains my day's end,
Provision and sharing, good gifts You did send.

[6] Many are saying, "Who will
show us *any* good?"
Lift up the light of Your countenance upon us, O LORD!

Contentions, death rattles, from lives spun askew,
Question Your goodness, yet spurn Your renew.
Lift the light higher! Perhaps they may see,
Your light heals their blindness;
Your face makes us free.

[7] You have put gladness in my
heart,
More than when their grain and new wine abound.

Luxuriant delight wells up from within,
The wine of Your joy washes out all my sin.
No lesser rival shall pirate my pleasure,
My spirit is nourished by You to full measure.

[8] In peace I will both lie down
and sleep,
For You alone, O LORD, make me to dwell in safety.

Your calm I will feel in the still of this night,
Peace comes in knowing with You I am right.
Solace I find in the midst of the storm,
My eyes gently close now, in You safe and warm.

You are not alone. Relax into your night. Know that life may not be perfect, but there is a peace that passes understanding. Know you are with One capable of surrounding you this night. You are held.

Taking Reflections with You

This psalm can mirror a day's anxiety and then create space to let it go.

Be clear about what has distracted you this day, demanding your attention. Let it go.

- Consider how you have tried to appear to people today.
- Shed all that is not true to you.
- Listen to the inward voices, urges, and anxieties.
- Discern all that is coming from your expectations and others.
- Let the Spirit attune you to the hospitality of God.
- Let the Spirit speak to your heart.

Behind the pavilion of peace, find a pool of reflection.

- Reflecting your feelings, what *images or words* touched you in this psalm? What might you embrace? What might you release?
- Next, explore what this psalm says *about* God. Did you discover more of the presence of God in this psalm? What do you hear his heart caring about?
- Now, ask what the psalm says *about you*. What sense did you have of the intrusion of others into your life? What anxiety is creating a sore spot for you?
- Finally, ask what this psalm says about *your relationship with* God. Can you live in the tension of wild and challenging days and then find restful nights of healing prayer? Do you have a vision of what being held might do for you?
- What is the LORD *saying to you* as you focus on listening? Let the Spirit open your ears to the voice of God. He is the God who speaks. Listening is the acknowledgment that allows you to receive. Refer to the psalm for words to ignite the listening.
- What do you want to *say back*? Continue with prayer as a calming conversation.

We use a pillow for comfort, to align our head and body with the bed. Let this psalm "pillow you" into a restful night.

Final Embrace

Slip gently from crashing waves of worry and regret toward echoes of sleep.

Distressed.
Fading light.
Getting undressed.
What a mess.
A day now passed.
Shoulders tight.
Temples on fire.
Such pain and stress.
Questions.
Delusions.
Convolutions.
Scheming illusions.
Perplexing intrusions.
A ray of light.
Glimpse of bright.
Sounds of soothing quiet.
Face of grace.
In my place.
Awakened healing place.
You speak.
My name.
Beloved.
My heart.
Never the same.
Your loyal love.
My drift to You.
Dreams.
Confidence.
In You.

Sit with this waterfall of words to find confidence in the One who touches hearts and births dreams.

Psalm 5

Seeking God with the Sunrise

In the morning, LORD, you hear my voice;
in the morning I lay my requests before you
and wait expectantly.
(Psalm 5:3 NIV)

Surveying the Garden

Some mornings, we crave support.

This psalm may provide what you need, expressing a desperate cry for resolve. The challenge you feel is likely not a result of your present needs but rather a consequence of a state you are experiencing that is possibly not because of your needs but because you have endured past hardships and experiences.

Other people's "perspectives" may come crashing down on you like cold waves. Being subjected to other people's lies can leave you feeling betrayed, disrespected, threatened, marginalized, and overwhelmed by a torrent of other negative emotions. The lie is in their inability to see your heart; they see what they want to see—whatever they see, it is not you.

You find yourself at a loss for words, even to pray—so you wait and shrink away in silence.

With the first glimmer of the rising sun, this place in the garden opens to welcome its light, dispelling the entombing clouds.

And then, like the presence of a cherished friend, the gift of kindness encircles you. You are becoming attuned to the garden's grace; new mercies greet you every morning.

He has heard your cry for help. He says, "I am here for you. Come walk with Me, and I will listen." May his compassion wash away the bitterness from your tired and weary soul.

Into the Garden with God

Begging God for help may happen every day. Or we may have stopped asking.

God may care enough about us not to give us the answers that would destroy us. But he gives us what we need to move us to health.

In Acts 3, we find the Spirit at work through Peter and John. They were heading to the temple to pray. Continuing the healing ministry that Jesus called them to share, they came across someone in need.

A lame man was pleading for alms; his is a desperate prayer to his fellow humans to help him meet his needs. Peter redirected the man from his immediate needs and gave him something he needed more deeply. Ultimately, the scripture reveals that we rely on others to find answers to our pain.

I invite you to step into this story (as an observer). Share the path and the moment.

> Now Peter and John were going up to the temple at the ninth
> *hour*, the hour of prayer. 2 And a man who had been unable to
> walk from birth was being carried, whom they used to set down
> every day at the gate of the temple which is called Beautiful, in
> order *for him* to beg for charitable gifts from those entering the
> temple *grounds*. 3 When he saw Peter and John about to go into
> the temple *grounds*, he *began* asking to receive a charitable
> gift. 4 But Peter, along with John, looked at him intently and
> said, "Look at us!" 5 And he gave them his attention, expecting to
> receive something from them. 6 But Peter said, "I do not have
> silver and gold, but what I do have I give to you: In the name of
> Jesus Christ the Nazarene, walk!"
>
> (Acts 3:1–6 NASB)

This story and this psalm call us to discover our deepest needs and who can meet them.

God calls to us, "Look at Me!" He gives us what we need. That is, to share our journey with God, allowing him to guide us and meet our needs.

Picture the wandering path of your life and awaken to the presence of the Spirit leading you through the twists and turns. Ahead, you will be securely guided and protected as you walk alongside God, who strides through the garden in the cool of the day.

Visions of Paradise

This pathway washes away the night's shadows to stir up joy as you approach the Father's house of love.

Along the Garden Path

This psalm's pathway is a place to listen and for emotional release. It is the path of honest conversations.

You wait attentively, knowing that the eternal God will take time to listen to you. You have been pummeled by the merciless rhythm of the previous days. You are drained as you face this new day. You are consumed with pain and discontent. You are needing strength. You are bent double from inner turmoil. But you know there is solace ahead. You are waiting to release a torrent of grief. You hope the muck and dross inside you will be absorbed and made pristine again by the Lord, who promises to transform the raging flood into a serene pool.

You are not calm. You feel the urge to release. The relief waits for you beyond the gate, even as you stumble and falter toward the resolution you know is coming. Look ahead and see Someone running to meet you. Take that step and be ready for that moment a few steps away, shielded in the deepest embrace.

If you have a groan or something to beg for at this moment, let it begin to slip out.

Indwelling the Garden

Hear the surround of birds awakening you to a new day, unspoiled and filled with light.

The first glow of morning reveals what was cold and hidden. The silence of the night is broken, and the cover of darkness is dispersed. Let warmth thaw your soul as grace flows over your whole being, and you begin to feel alive.

1 Give ear to my words, O LORD,
Consider my groaning.

Listen again, oh Lover of Lives,
To the garden of thoughts that in me strives,
They're spread awry before You now,
Needing re-patterning by Your plow.

2 Heed the sound of my cry for help, my King and my God,
For to You I pray.

Attend the wounds that ache my soul,
The turmoiled path that I must stroll,
I humbly lift my weakened cries
To You, my Master, Mentor, and Prize.

3 In the morning, O LORD, You
will hear my voice;
In the morning I will order *my*
prayer to You and *eagerly*
watch.

I rise with the dawn to sit here still,
My ears and heart You gently fill,
My half-breathed whisper reveals deep
needs,
That on Your answer I may feed.

4 For You are not a God who takes
pleasure in wickedness;
No evil dwells with You.

Rebellion and brokenness pain Your all,
Divine teardrops, like rain, do fall.
No fracturing thought sojourns Your
way,
Your bright inner life brings glory to
play.

5 The boastful shall not stand
before Your eyes;
You hate all who do iniquity.

Persons who poison their lives with
hate,
Meet their match at Your front
gate.
Their polluting refuting of Your goodwill,
You bring to silence—Your peaceful
still.

6 You destroy those who speak
falsehood;
The LORD abhors the man of
bloodshed and deceit.

The final blow to dark is light,
All lying ends when pierced by Your
sight.
Abuse repulses Your healing heart,
Pretense melts; You're its counterpart.

7 But as for me, by Your abundant
lovingkindness I will enter
Your house,
At Your holy temple I will bow in
reverence for You.

Engulfed by kindness, like an ocean's swell,
I enter Your presence, so that in You
I dwell.
Now, in Your refuge of living fire,
Adoration ignites with love's blazing
conspire.

8 O LORD, lead me in Your
righteousness because of
my foes;
Make Your way straight
before me.

Safe in the wildness of Your space,
Protected from the crooked pace,
All diversions are made straight in You,
Fearlessly, I walk, as we share the
view.

[9] There is nothing reliable in
what they say;
Their inward part is destruction itself.
Their throat is an open grave;
They flatter with their tongue.

The slippery path I will avoid,
Troubling murmurers choose a life devoid,
Entombed in deception, blind in their brew,
They collapse on themselves, their compass askew.

[10] Hold them guilty, O God;
By their own devices let them fall!
In the multitude of their transgressions thrust them out,
For they are rebellious against You.

Stop the rebellion, their wildfire ablaze,
Their raging riot, squelch at first stage.
Hold them at bay, those out to do harm,
Discipline justly with Your mighty arm.

[11] But let all who take refuge in You be glad,
Let them ever sing for joy;
And may You shelter them,
That those who love Your name may exult in You.

Charmed life is enjoyed in Your sheltering tent,
Your zest begins where our strength is spent.
Voices shall rise to blazon Your name,
Heart-love will flow in joyous exclaim.

[12] For it is You who blesses the righteous man,
O LORD,
You surround him with favor as with a shield.

Your encircling enfolds, keeping trouble at bay,
Embracing Your children while the oceans play.
Caressed on Your fingertips by love so sure,
Your grace is my shield, encompassed, secure.

Envision your day with bravery born of the Spirit's empowerment.
You have a companion in the triune God—
the Father is fond of you,
the Son promises to be with you,
and the Spirit comes alongside to help as needed.

Taking Reflections with You

Reflect on this psalm as a rest stop. You are never on this pathway alone, but you may need to pay attention.

The night is fading, and the first step of the new day is accepting that you want to be alive today—feel the grounding; maybe it is holy ground if you let it be.

As you sit at the rest stop, consider wearing this psalm as a cloak of compassion, shielding you from the struggles and covering you with courage.

- What *images or words* stand out, touching on what you are feeling? What needs to cry out in you?
- What does this psalm say *about God*, and can you let him tell you what he sees? How did God show up for you in this psalm? Do you feel he cares about you?
- How did this psalm reveal emotions that dwell or swell up in *you*? What resentments reside in you, like weeds that need attention? What touch of kindness are you looking for?
- What opened up for you in understanding *your relationship with* God? Can you see God's companionship as part of your walk along your path? Does companionship matter, or do you think you should handle life by yourself?
- What is the LORD whispering to you as he addresses you in this psalm? Let God's compassionate voice bathe your mind, embrace you, heal the hurt, and calm the unsettling of the unknown.
- What do you want to *say or give back*? Say it out loud. Continue with prayer as an embracing hug emerges around you and sounds of satisfaction are released from you!

As the sun rises, put on the glasses of grace. See God's gift—redeeming broken situations and bringing solutions beyond your comprehension.

Final Embrace

Take a moment to stretch and feel your sore muscles or bruised memories of yesterday. Now breathe in hope for restorative limberness today.

Read slowly and feel the words as they slip out, laden with emotions needing names.

Listening.
Sighing.
Preparing.
Aware of lies.
Muttering.
Puttering.
Pondering why.
Those wayward eyes.
Feeling tension.
Wanting intervention.
Releasing apprehension.
Mood divided.
Fragments of truth.
Kaleidoscopic meditations.
Some fight, some light.
Hoping to see You.
Homeward to Your draw.
I sense the final straw.
I need an Ebenezer stone.[1]
Your help alone.
The rock of redeeming.
Shedding off scheming.
A canopy of kindness.
The path to your Royal Highness.
Exultant breath.
Released from death.
Springing with favor.
Blessed forever.
Pathways of pleasure.
Sojourning.
Recovered.
Covered.
Hid with You.
Safe.

[1] Stone of help

Psalm 6

Encountering Embodied Angst

Have mercy on me, Lord, for I am faint;
heal me, Lord, for my bones are in agony.
(Psalm 6:2 NIV)

Surveying the Garden

Exhaustion includes both bodily and emotional vulnerability.

As we approach this psalm, we feel the fragility of our humanity. We are not in control.

This psalm is a prayer spilling out from hours of anguish. The words take us deep into the challenge of living in the shadow of disease and defeat.

You may want to join these impassioned pleas. You may think the pain and pressures you experience come from God or are just part of life. The point is to move toward healing and not blame. Feel what disturbs you right now. Prepare to find solidarity with the God who suffers with you.

We have failing bodies and experience discouraging moments. Accept that, and surrender the light of grace, finding solace in the arms that answer your heart's cry.

The Faithful God accompanies you with his promise of healing presence. This psalm permits you to cry, "Remember me; I am spent." This honesty is a form of humility and holiness. Embracing the grace that meets us offers us the promise of health. We are never self-improved.

Jesus knows this place well and welcomes you with his tears and scars. We all feel moments and seasons of loss, pain, and angst. Hope is in the promise that "today is not the end."

Hear the response: "I do remember you. I care about your whole being, body, and soul. I will be with you to the end and beyond." Feel his heart of compassion holding your weary soul.

Into the Garden with God

Jesus spent time in the garden of suffering. He knows where to go when the body fails and friends have failed you.

As we face our challenges, having friends is life-sustaining. Finding ourselves deserted is devastating and maddening. When we are not supported with companionship, we begin to yearn for what is missing. In the resounding void, anger and emptiness stir up a heart-shattering storm.

In John's gospel, Jesus approaches his death. Today's psalm echoes what springs from his lips:

> **"Now My soul has become troubled; and what am I to say? 'Father, save Me from this hour'? But for this purpose I came to this hour. 28 Father, glorify Your name." Then a voice came out of heaven: "I have both glorified *it*, and will glorify *it* again."**
> (John 12:27–28 NASB)

Like David in the Psalms, Jesus has a troubled soul and an honest cry. His agony does not end with defeat but with hope. He knows his Father's grace will win the day. His Father has a deep heart. In the midst of trouble, our hearts find confidence in him.

Jesus knows how despair and displeasure seep into our fractured lives. We need his heart to lift our eyes to refocus.

Jesus is the Healer of our lives. He invites you to look at him as you are collapsed in confusion, feeling alone here in the part of the garden where the wild things roam. He says, "You are not alone; I have wept here too."

Visions of Paradise

On this couch, you will find a place of connection. You can explore your vulnerability and discover your value to the Healer of your whole being. He joins you to create a safe space to look at the turmoil inside. It is safe to unlock the pressures that swarm like insects inside. Here you are restored, hearing a voice to give you the energy to take steps of courage.

Along the Garden Path

This is a very bodily psalm.

As you prepare to enter, feelings of weariness, exhaustion, being at death's door, grief, and feeling the weight of God's displeasure as guilt create an intuitive sense of feeling overwhelmed, maybe forgotten, possibly even punished.

The cry erupting in the psalm, and maybe you, is for deliverance.

Along this path, focus on what has made you recognize God as your most steadfast companion. Let fear melt into acceptance and relief.

God is attentive to what has been happening as you are plagued by pests. He sees when you stumble emotionally. He feels the ache in your bones.

But within this psalm, you will discover restoration. Imagine a luxurious couch that invites you to weep, soothe your weary bones, and be comforted. The graceful scent of eucalyptus permeates the air. You sense the healing properties, and you breathe in as it calms your nerves.

But mostly, become aware that Jesus is there. He, too, has been weeping, mostly for the world he loves. But his sorrow turns to joy as he sees you.

Take a breath and move your body. See if you can feel any aches and pains. Think of the story in your head from last week. Feel your disappointments and how they weigh on you. Now enter and settle into that waiting place of renewal.

Indwelling the Garden

As the shadows lengthen and the curtain of night falls, attune your heart and eyes to see deeply as you enter the calm of this psalm.

1 O LORD, do not rebuke me in Your
anger,
Nor chasten me in Your wrath.

Childlike, humble, before You I kneel,
I need Your touch, but squirm to feel
My failure's bruise may be renewed,
With mercy, let my sin be viewed.

2 Be gracious to me, O LORD, for I *am*
pining away;
Heal me, O LORD, for my bones are
dismayed.

Drowning, I dredge in my misery.
Please whisper Your availability,
Be present in this gloom of need,
My back is bent, a broken reed.

3 And my soul is greatly dismayed;
But You, O LORD—how long?

My inner strength is all but gone,
I sink exhausted, awaiting the dawn
To bring refreshing strength and song.
But my voice now aches, "How
long?"

4 Return, O LORD, rescue my soul;
Save me because of Your
lovingkindness.

Revisit me in this lonely hour,
Restore again with compassion's
power.
Make me whole with Your great love,
Liberate my caged soul's dove.

5 For there is no mention of You in
death;
In Sheol who will give You thanks?

While my lips still praise Your name
I'll speak Your wonder with tongue
aflame.
Beyond, in death, all words are still,
Gratitude fades to blackest chill.

6 I am weary with my sighing;
Every night I make my bed swim,
I dissolve my couch with my tears.

Spent from thrashing in the night,
A pool of tears bespeaks my
plight.
The taste of salt, the cry-worn throat,
Surrounded by my tear-filled moat.

7 My eye has wasted away with grief;
It has become old because of all my
adversaries.

My blurried eyes are washed with
grief
Stealing my vision as a thief.
Invaded by my enemy's prodding
Leaves me battered with fears
marauding.

8 Depart from me, all you who do
iniquity,
For the LORD has heard the voice of
my weeping.

"Let me be," you encroaching foes,
Who wish my life would decompose.
A hand has reached to calm my night,
My Master comes and melts my
fright.

9 The LORD has heard my
supplication,
The LORD receives my prayer.

LORD, I know You heard my cry,
Gave gentle peace to close my eyes.
I asked, You gave me what I need,
Your full attention; now, You
lead.

10 All my enemies will be ashamed and
greatly dismayed;
They shall turn back, they will
suddenly be ashamed.

Victory's gift has finally come,
The challengers kneel to Him who
won,
Defeat has come to those thought strong,
Those out of tune with Your sweet
song.

The Spirit goes with you through this prayer, now ready to face the same journey—but not alone. You are mending with an energy not your own. Allow the Spirit's presence to overcome your health's diminished vitality. Hand over the emotional bruises from those who have shown themselves not to be your friends. Move on. Accept yourself as you are already accepted. Remember grace. Shed the shaming. Remember whose you are.

Taking Reflections with You

This psalm is much like a car wash. It brings awareness of the grime and grunge that covers your personal life. Its jets remove layers of complaint, and then its brushes turn and churn to release you from the memories and manifestations of failure.

The Spirit is here to renew and empower you, even covering you with the protective wax of divine freedom. It will make you shine inside and out. That is called glory. Release yourself into this inquiry of cleansing.

- What *images or words* touched on the challenges you are dealing with? What sentences give you permission to honestly let out what bothers you?
- What does this psalm reveal *about* God? Do you recognize any feelings you have about God that are confronted or confirmed? Do you sense he feels all your pains and is also the presence that will bring the final resolve to your suffering?
- How did this psalm expose the sensations and emotions that describe your bodily and emotional challenges? What did it reveal *about you*? Where do you go for renewal when you are discouraged? Or, is support from others missing in your life?
- What opened up for you in understanding *your relationship with* God? Can you hold both the pain of the moment and the confidence of God's healing purposes at the same time? Do you think you are failing in your relationship with God when you let out your complaints? Or can you see those as moments of the most open, trusting connection?
- Can you *hear God's voice* addressing you directly in this psalm? Try to let God's compassionate voice rinse your mind

and help you find courage in hearing his confident companionship.

- What do you want to *say back to him*? Be honest. Be direct. Let prayer today be a release from keeping your thoughts inside. Try to stop editing as you respond and speak fearlessly to free up body and soul for living graciously unbounded.

Let the memories of both the *irritations* and the *celebrations* of the good wash over you. Let the Spirit whisk away all distractions and whisper: "He sees you, he feels you, he waits with you until you are ready to step into this day with him."

Final Embrace

Feeling the bruises and aches of growing old can diminish our enjoyment of life. But refocusing on the memories and the celebrations yet to come can be a breath of renewal inside and out. Read as slowly as you are able, to receive the bouquet.

Disturbed.
Perturbed.
Wanting to be heard.
Corrected.
Dejected.
Anguishing.
Languishing.
Fading and failing.
Falling apart.
Wanting a new start.
I'm open.
Remember words You've spoken.
Need a cure.
Reassure.
Find secure.
Delivered from death's door.
Turning back from grief.
Need relief.
A reason for belief.
Waning like the moon.
Coyotes know my howl.
Sobbing voice.
Weeping eyes.
Thunderous cries.
Sorrow fills the skies.
Return.
Restore.
Heard once more.
Disgrace washed with grace.
Celebrate Your face.
Concrete.
Connect.
Intersect my pain.
Release.
Peace.

Psalm 7

Travail in Troubled Times

Bring to an end the violence of the wicked and make the righteous secure—you, the righteous God who probes minds and hearts.

(Psalm 7:9 NIV)

Surveying the Garden

Even close relationships can go awry. The result is emotional turmoil.

How do we shed the residue of slander, betrayal, unexplained enmity, or the grief of unresolved loss? How can we process our pain, searching to resolve the instability of being left in the dark in confusion?

Try using an "emotional thermometer" by saying to yourself, "I am at peace with everyone." Then, pause and consider whether this statement is true. Listen as your spirit communicates the exceptions to you. (Example: "That claim is a lie"; "hardly true"; "well, mostly"; or absolute yes—whatever comes!)

Now, we will attach some numbers. If you feel "I am at peace" is true, give yourself a 10 (corresponding to 98.6 for a proper body temperature, true = 10). Any other number shows your emotional temperature is off. If something is missing, give a lower number (hardly true = 1 to 5). If you are overheating mad, go for a number that reflects that (not true = –1 to –10). You may need more than one thermometer to assess different situations.

Let the meaning of the exceptions (those not 10) sink in. Accept that Jesus wants you to be *honest* rather than *fake* your feelings. This psalm is an opening step into his refuge.

Honesty is essential for moving toward wholeness. Where you have been attacked, where people have lied about you, you must acknowledge this in order to heal. Honest acknowledgment empowers you to be healthy instead of remaining a victim.

Acknowledging creates a sacred place. Honesty releases what robs you of joy. It provides a sheltering space to identify and cleanse the toxic pain. You are going to move now and restore your primary connection with the healing God.

Jesus will walk with you now as an advocate and scout, giving you eyes to see a Securer waiting ahead.

Jesus gives you a trustful gaze. He looks into your struggling soul. He invites you to consider his offer: "All will be well; take my hand and let's bravely confront and transform the difficult emotions within you."

Into the Garden with God

Jesus understands what it is like to be misrepresented, judged, and betrayed. He knows this as a common human experience. He feels you, and this psalm may reflect your feelings, where you are caught in the tension.

Jesus's ministry continues to set things right in a world gone astray. He encountered selfish people who could not help but cause pain. We meet these people too.

Jesus does not want us to be vengeful or self-righteous in response. Despite the wreckage of failed friendships, he maintains a steady gaze on the horizon, unwavering in his hope for a brighter future. He sees through these challenges to a hopeful end, even amidst failed friendships.

> **"Blessed are you when *people* insult you and persecute you, and falsely say all kinds of evil against you because of Me. [12] Rejoice and be glad, for your reward in heaven is great; for in the same way they persecuted the prophets who were before you."**
> (Matthew 5:11–12 NASB)

Jesus could stay focused on restoring friendship and dealing with enemies. He still continues to bless others, embodying grace through his unconditionally accepting presence, even toward the undeserving.

Some of the humans in our story are very fallible. We must accept them as they are but not be drawn into their dysfunction, and know that we are not stuck with them forever.

This psalm petitions for God's wrath and judgment. *Wrath* is a tricky word, but it is about correction. It illustrates God's burning love coming forth and breaking all obstacles that impede that love. Wrath breaks the chains, leading to freedom or ending the abuse of another. God says yes to love and no to violence.

Jesus wraps you in a robe of rejoicing, saying, "Joy is my gift. Step through the gate and come join Me on that bench, and let's cast out what haunts you."

Visions of Paradise

The bench beyond the gate serves as a place of contemplation and rest. Inside the gate is a healing place for setting things right by aligning with the glory of the garden and the Gardener.

Along the Garden Path

We are entering the garden gate of this stormy psalm.

In ancient times, the judges sat at the city gate. They had no courtroom to adjudicate long and contentious trials. Every day, the wise of the city came to arbitrate over the affairs of the people who needed restitution at every level.

This psalm escorts us inside the gate; we yearn to be embraced, needing restitution.

We will move through our present pain and seek lasting peace. We will discern what hinders our peace and reshape our relationship to what binds us.

Freedom will follow as we realign with the One who heals our hearts.

Step gently through the gate. Focus on feeling your pain while finding freedom in being honest. Seek sincere, constructive ways to transcend your resistance and exhaustion.

Indwelling the Garden

The very thought of old friends and enemies can feel like thunderstorms and lightning flashes of past hurts. Voices of judgment, criticism, and betrayal may feel like sudden strikes to your soul.

You need safety. Enter now and be open to the steps of releasing.

1 O LORD my God, in You I have taken refuge;
Save me from all those who pursue me, and deliver me,

Oh, may I find my hiding place,
Lost in the arms of You.
Help me in my time of need,
Protect from those who pursue.

2 Or he will tear my soul like a lion,
Dragging me away, while there is none to deliver.

The claws of a roar now shred my night,
My heart is ruthlessly gripped,
Torn and battered, tugged along,
All calm is hopelessly stripped.

3 O LORD my God, if I have done this,
If there is injustice in my hands,

I fear the backward glance to find
That I have caused offense.
Have I, unconsciously, acted cruel,
Built an aggrieving fence?

4 If I have rewarded evil to my friend,
Or have plundered him who without cause was my adversary,

Have I returned a jab for a joy
And missed an outstretched hand?
My blindness may have caused some harm,
So a friend against me now stands.

5 Let the enemy pursue my soul and overtake it;
And let him trample my life down to the ground
And lay my glory in the dust. [*Selah*]

I humbly lay my failure down,
My pride must be undone.
Let my self-made glory dim,
With my trust in You begun.
[I rest in You]

6 Arise, O LORD, in Your anger;
Lift up Yourself against the rage of my adversaries,
And arouse Yourself for me; You have appointed judgment.

Arise, Oh Master of all souls,
Defend the poor and meek.
You stand for truth against all lies;
Your justice now I seek.

7 Let the assembly of the peoples encompass You,
And over them return on high.

Gathered round as little ones,
Let the nations come.
You, the giver of all life,
Exalted One become.

8 The LORD judges the peoples;
Vindicate me, O LORD, according to my righteousness and my integrity that is in me.

Wisely weigh the wayward ones,
To find a balanced stand.
With Your wisdom, bring relief,
My honor's in Your hand.

9 O let the evil of the wicked come to an end, but establish the righteous;
For the righteous God tries the hearts and minds.

Finish now the raging mob,
Their ruinous danger at play.
You who settle human ills,
Restore the just pathway.

10 My shield is with God,
Who saves the upright in heart.

My safeguard sure is in Your grasp,
Held throughout the day.
My tender core can finally rest,
In Your embrace I'll stay.

11 God is a righteous judge,
And a God who has indignation every day.

Sage foresight always flows from You,
Outshining lesser lights,
Your love burns like summer's noon,
Revealing human plights.

12 If a man does not repent, He will sharpen His sword;
He has bent His bow and made it ready.

13 He has also prepared for Himself deadly weapons;
He makes His arrows fiery shafts.

With a surgeon's skill to extract all ill,
Your scalpel's ready raised,
Armed to root out cancer's harm,
Prepared with searching ways.
No hostile flesh shall stand its ground
When He comes in to cure.
His remedy is always full,
The medicine burning pure.

14 Behold, he travails with wickedness,
And he conceives mischief and brings forth falsehood.

A rebellious fool in delusion fights,
Foiled by eyes grown dim,
Oblivious of who against him stands,
Spinning his own whirlwind.

15 He has dug a pit and hollowed it out,
And has fallen into the hole which he made.

He sets a trap to catch his foe,
A dark and fearsome hole,
But in his clumsy conniving,
He slips and snares his soul.

16 His mischief will return upon his own head,
And his violence will descend upon his own pate.

All the injury he has caused,
Will haunt him in the end,
The sun shall scald his withered skull,
Alone without a friend.

17 I will give thanks to the LORD according to His righteousness
And will sing praise to the name of the LORD Most High.

My grateful hands shall stretch out wide,
I'll walk with wisdom's stride.
My voice shall leap o'er hill to dale,
While joyful at Your side.

Try stretching your hands out wide, like spreading sails of gratitude. Let the wind of the Spirit sweep through you. Feel the color of warmth light you up like a lantern in a dark place. Let gratitude penetrate the shadows. Let hidden beauty reverse the heaviness and make the moment light.

Taking Reflections with You

Contemplation resembles polishing a precious stone. You turn the ideas over, allowing the friction to bring out the beauty of what is hidden beneath the rough surface.

In this reflection, allow for the challenges faced in this psalm to be seen and heard, and see what emotions they mirror back to you.

- What *words* hit a nerve or sweet spot? What experiences resonated with your past?
- What was revealed *about God*? Where did you feel God in the midst of your suffering? How was the heart of God present to you?
- How did this psalm mirror *your life*? What became clear about *who you are* amid challenges that came to mind? What insights are you discovering about *who you are* in response to this psalm?
- What is opening for you in understanding *your relationship with God*? Is your urge for justice showing up (Get 'em, God! Protect me!)? Is your relationship with God affected by your challenges (Where are you?)? Are you at peace with God, or do you want something more to feel satisfied in your relationship?
- Are you learning to *hear the Living God address you* as a beloved person in this psalm? ("I am your hiding place. . . .")
- What do you want to reply to his offer to be with you and for you?

How are your head and heart doing?

Do you have a story to share with friends as a result of this time of reflection? Consider sharing what stood out to you today with a friend or family member. Sharing brings connection, and everyone benefits.

Healing is a renewing process. Read and feel the pain. As you finish, begin to sense the return of the pulse of love.

Final Embrace

Breathe deep to be ready to exhale through these words to let the past be released and carried away by the wind. Let that breath out. Now stop and breathe, maybe with each line. Let the breaths carry you to the end.

Slandered.
Surrounded.
Hounded.
Seeking refuge.
Life in a centrifuge.
Urgency.
Deliver me.
Will I ever be free?
From hypocrisy?
Wanting to be friendly.
Susceptible to leniency.
To undeserving enemies.
Those who hunt me.
Pursuing.
Overtaking.
Trampling.
Humiliating.
Lord, do something.
Find a different way.
Let your justice play.
Gather nations.
Bring transformations.
Reveal Your habitation.
Creation's true foundation.
Work integrity's emotions.
Wrap me with Your presence.
Beyond all pretense.
Be my defense.
Show Your forgiveness.
Let Your indignation.
Embrace the marginalized.
For those born penalized.
Who cannot manage.
Oppressed by carnage.
From those who tarnish.
Who labor in lying.
Conceived in heart-harming.
Pregnant with disrupting.
Birthing falsifying.
Spawning wrongdoing.
Maturing their mischief.
Life in the pits.
Living a counterfeit.
Please, show me Your benefit.
Help me to enter it.
'Til my song is commensurate.
Attuning.
Aligning.
Adoring.

(Big breath of release in, then out, . . . rest).

Psalm 8

Creation's Contexts of Cherishing

LORD, our Lord, how majestic is your name in
all the earth!
You have set your glory in the heavens.
(Psalm 8:1 NIV)

Surveying the Garden

Now, we consider the meaning of life. This includes the meaning of your life.

Meaning comes from contexts. This psalm equips you with lenses to focus on where and whose you are. If you read carefully, you will see these layers of our existence displayed:

The largest context in life is God, the Creator of the universe.

The second context is the created universe, the work of God's hands.

Within the universe, we live on a small planet, fashioned for life.

Humans, created in God's image, constitute the field of human persons, intended to love God and one another.

Finally, animals are created as another stratum of living beings. They are resources for humans to manage responsibly and also intended for his and our delight.

Today, we are looking at who you are in this big God-fashioned garden. It is so big that it echoes from the opening chapters of Genesis. We will observe God's peerless work in creating the heavens and the earth—and you.

This psalm makes us aware of what is beyond our eyes. In this moment, we are in his presence, entering the garden. Proceed with wonder. As Einstein said, "The most beautiful thing we can experience is the mysterious. It is the source of all true art and science. He to whom this emotion is a stranger, who can no longer pause to wonder and stand rapt in awe, is as good as dead: his eyes are closed" (Einstein 1931, 6).

As you read, questions may arise, such as "Who am I that anyone should care about me?" The question "Who am I?" is a profoundly important compass for our inquiry, guiding our search for meaning. God is committed to answering that question.

This psalm opens our eyes to the realization that at different levels all created things, including you, echo the Creator's relational way of being.

All creation lives in dynamic, integrated harmony and depends on God's continuing creativity. You are connected in profound ways.

All that surrounds us is so different from us, yet so familiar. We all resonate with a glory that is the handiwork of God's grandeur. We are living things by God's gifting.

The Creator God stands ready to open your eyes. He wants you to see that he is the Artist who made you and all you can survey. Moreover, he has time to be with you; you are his cherished child and friend.

Into the Garden with God

Jesus walked with children who seemed to know *who* they were with. The children honored him. When the religious leaders tried to stop the children, Jesus quoted from Psalm 8:2. The leaders said to Jesus,

> "Do You hear what these *children* are saying?" And Jesus said to them, "Yes. Have you never read, 'FROM THE MOUTHS OF INFANTS AND NURSING BABIES YOU HAVE PREPARED PRAISE FOR YOURSELF'?"
> (Matthew 21:16 NASB)

The wise and the religious often miss what is going on. But children can see with wonder, curiosity, and delight.

In its own way, each thing in creation proclaims the honor due its Creator. Our task is to observe with our hearts and listen with curiosity and gratitude to develop an attitude of worship for the Artist.

When we set aside "what we think God is like" and begin to recognize him as he shows up, we get out of our heads and into the reality in front of us.

He is not "the art" we call the world. Rather importantly, the world's beauty and story shout his praises and point to him—to enjoy him forever. He is in the garden with us, dressed in clothes ready to get dirty. He is ever attentive to the needs of gardens and our lives.

He cares for the rest of the world but has time to pull weeds in your own garden. He yearns to discover what brings you joy today so he can share in your happiness, cherish it, and be there for you when things get tough.

This psalm is an invitation to become a child again, to marvel anew at how the Master Artist's touch extends to all visible things and beyond. See how small you are yet how appreciated you feel as he walks the garden with you on the way to the observatory and says, "Let's go be astonished!"

Visions of Paradise

Having seen the stars, galaxies, and the vastness of all that spreads with wonder into infinity, step back and recognize that the Person who made them values you with endless delight. Let out a "Wow!" as you see the stars twinkling, the snow falling, or the spring buds bursting out. Then, hear him say "Wow," looking right at you. Say "Wow" back.

Along the Garden Path

If you pay attention to the path before you, your heart will gain eyes to see expansive new depths of God's consideration for you:

- As you begin to walk the *garden path*, slow down and recognize that he always carefully creates a place for you to walk toward and with him.
- Slowly glance side to side, expanding your vision from the path, to experience it as part of a *tended garden*. It is not here by accident. He has created an environment to build anticipation—it was made for you to enjoy with him.
- Let your mind expand with a new perspective on the *whole world*. He designed a miracle of life that defies explanation, and he wants you to live in it with wonder.
- Glancing higher, see the *moon*, day or night, shining because it dances with the bright *sun's* light. Each celestial light, in its own way, works at illuminating and nurturing all within its scope at his command.
- Beyond, unseen in the day, the *stars and their galaxies* stretch across the *universe* as a symphony of splendor. They come out in the night to glimpse the greatness of God.
- One final step: Let your heart hear from beyond—catch the heart of the Living God who made the universe. He animates everything, bringing it to life in a flurry of movement. The Father's creative heart embraces the universe. Through the Son, God's loving presence is daily revealed in its majesty and mystery. This miraculous moment blossoms with the Creator Spirit's whispered grace.

In the midst of this dancing universe, you may feel small.

You may be stirred as you become aware that the Creator is with you.

The path, the garden, the world, the solar system, and the universe are all made by One God in three Persons who had you in mind.

Let your heart be aroused, waiting to know the delight of being loved, nurtured, and given the joy of being alive and attuned to the Creator.

In a glance, try to take it all in as one grand kaleidoscope, one universe layered with complexity. You are inextricably linked to the larger whole, interacting with unseen complexities.

Then consider this—you are profoundly valuable even when you feel invisible.

You are ready to enter the path. Sense the exuberance of the embrace of it all as God makes you an observer and participant in it and says, "Let me expand your tender heart with my gentle touch. Let me open your eyes to see more."

Indwelling the Garden

Feel the breath of the Creator. Hear the silent voices of all creation honoring the One who made it all, praising the King of hearts, who brings our focus to the beauty and value of it all as his masterpiece.

1 O LORD, our LORD,
How majestic is Your name in all the earth,
Who have displayed Your splendor above the heavens!

Oh King of Hearts, who tends our hearts,
What brilliance shares Your honor's fame?
The earth adorned with grandeur's flair
Celebrates Your excellent Name.

2 From the mouth of infants and nursing babes
You have established strength
Because of Your adversaries,
To make the enemy and the revengeful cease.

From day of birth You give us mirth
To intricately shape our spring.
Your peace is final as the sleep
That nestles within Your wing.

3 When I consider Your heavens, the work of Your fingers,
The moon and the stars, which You have ordained;

I gaze on the infinite sweep of Your touch,
The stars and the sunset, they thrill,
I walk in the moonlight, and You hold my hand,
By the other the Milky Way twirls.

4 What is man that You take thought of him,
And the son of man that You care for him?

How can You care for small human souls
While keeping the universe in place?
Your delicate offspring You tenderly feed,
Why do You gift us this grace?

5 Yet You have made him a little lower than God,
And You crown him with glory and majesty!

Value is given to rest by Your side,
An honor bestowed, not what's due.
You clothe us in beauty, readied to bloom,
Your cherish engulfs us, endows love anew.

6 You make him to rule over the works of Your hands;
You have put all things under his feet,

You call us to care, to steward the earth,
Though we are but seed on the soil.
You, the true Gardener, make the fields thrive,
We can but gratefully toil.

7 All sheep and oxen,
And also the beasts of the field,

All the fine animals graze the green hills,
Never a thought of strife.
Content in the care of provision full shared,
The simple, abundant wildlife.

8 The birds of the heavens and the fish of the sea,
Whatever passes through the paths of the seas.

Wings fill the air, the fowl-keeper is You,
The ocean is full of finned life,
We careful do tend, with You as our Guide
Fending off all worry and strife.

9 O LORD, our LORD,
How majestic is Your name in all the earth!

Oh King of Hearts who tends our hearts,
What brilliance shares Your honor's fame?
The earth adorned with grandeur's flair,
Celebrates Your excellent Name.

Let the eyes of your heart be opened and hear his Name resonate in your spirit. Release into his love; you are secure in his presence, not alone. You are a beloved child made to be held and enjoyed in this life together.

Taking Reflections with You

Trust your intuition. Become alive to the One who sustains you physically and personally. This is how wisdom, shaped by God, fashions us and makes us grow in awareness.

Let the words of this psalm be a window of blessing and meaning, opening you to the awe of this moment, enabling you to embrace your best loving self in his liberating presence.

- What *images* in the psalm are making you feel alive?
- How are you seeing and sensing God in a new way? Describe how he is a less distant, more present Creator. How would it feel to believe he watches over you and gives you true freedom, not by going away, but by always being with you?
- How did this psalm expand *your life*? Do you have a new understanding of *who you are* in the eyes and heart of God? What do you see afresh about the meaning of your life within all God has made and cares for?
- Think about how you are becoming more connected and vibrant in *your relationship with God*. What emotion do you notice as you read this psalm, seeing what is now possible as you come alive with him each day? What is missing in you when he is absent from the story of your day (losing love's context)?
- What does he say delights him about you? Can you *hear him* affirm who you are, just as you are? ("My child, I delight in the way you . . .")
- What *words of gratitude* might come to mind when you think about the Creator of the universe taking this time to be with you? What do you want to say to him? Can you let "Wow!" become a prayer that permeates your life?

Final Embrace

Feel the emotions as you inhale each following word, like considerately breathing in the embrace of a cherished friend. It is more than arms and more than words; in the grip, you feel the heart's embrace.

Overwhelmed.
Observing.
Echoing the wonder.
Valued.
Vastness.
Unleashed magnitudes.
Feeling dwarfed.
But You.
Center of all,
Containing all.
Your name on everyone's lips.
Creation spoken.
Innocent children see and say.
Arrogant enemies are kept at bay.
Still, before a spinning display.
Attentive now.
Remembering how.
You promised.
You visited.
You cherished.
Why?
Mud made men.
Dust to dust.
Yet masterpieces.
Frailty.
Extraordinary.
Unbound complexity.
Concerned for the seen world.
Stewards.
Fish friends,
Fowl friends.
Glory streams from heaven,
In feathers, flesh, and fins.
Sustained.
The impossible possibility.
Life named.
Wild and tamed.
Graced.
Responsible.
Awakened.
Expanded horizons.
Bigger contexts.
Nature.
Universe.
Speaking God.
Together.

Psalm 9

Grasping for God, Surrounded by Gangs

The Lord *is a refuge for the oppressed,*
a stronghold in times of trouble.
(Psalm 9:9 NIV)

Surveying the Garden

Deep gasps of gratitude re-center our attention.

Imagine this psalm as an exercise, giving us energy to jump and sing the songs of praise welling up inside us. Then, imagine a minute later, there on the floor we lie, exhausted by the tensions and interruptions of our daily routine, wishing to rise but unable to.

We must prepare our minds, hearts, and bodies, with hope, to respond.

As we walk through life, we discover we are not in control. We are limited by our own abilities. We also feel constrained by those who engage us daily with ill will.

With courage, we will show up again, submitting to God's just guidance. Justice means making things right. We can trust his lead; it will help us endure the garden's twists and turns.

And we will hit walls. Initially, we build barriers to protect ourselves, but they end up stopping us. "I am afraid of what will happen if I . . ." becomes a wall of resistance to shield ourselves. It ends up draining us of the courage to invest in self-giving love. We become our own fortress. But there is another who protects us.

Walls were built in ancient times to shelter from storms and threats. This psalm falls within that harboring type. It stands strong, even while the waves and winds whip in and around it. And we know the One who controls the winds. Unsurprisingly, when situations seem to gang up on us, we instinctively seek security elsewhere. But for us, God will always be that secure fortress.

Looking ahead, there will be a day when all will be calmed, the garden serene, the weeds removed, the sun shining, and the Master Gardener will bring all to its fulfilled fruition. This psalm gives us a glimpse of that day.

Today, ground your confidence in the Rock. Stand on that Rock and envision a different kind of day. Take the hand of Jesus as he invites you to walk with confidence through what lies ahead, saying, "I got you."

Into the Garden with God

Jesus knows about the need for rescue.

He left his disciples in a world transformed by the kingdom, whose fulfillment was yet to be realized. There was a lot of work to be done for the gospel to reconstruct what had deteriorated.

Paul was a rebuilder. When Paul stood in Athens on the hill called the Areopagus, or Mars Hill, it was a place of judgment and debate. Paul confronted the false gods of the philosophers and planted the good news of Jesus in their place.

Having portrayed Jesus to those gathered, Paul alluded to Psalm 9, saying,

> He [the true God] has set a day on which He will judge the world
> in righteousness through a Man whom He has appointed.
> (Acts 17:31 NASB)

Paul knew that the act would be to focus on the Living God. In that Greco-Roman culture, caught in the tangled vines of human wisdom, he could see that it would be left in ruins in the ages to come. But on that day, God was made present through Paul's preaching. God's corrective justice stood as a beacon of hope.

We still stand in hope today. As we enter the garden, we draw strength from what has already been fulfilled as we anticipate triumphs. He who promised is faithful.

Breathe in trust and confidence to fill your heart with hope. Then, exhale the frustration, vindictiveness, distress, and sense of abandonment that pummel and wear on you.

Feel him take your yearning hand in his and hear him say: "If you fall, I will hold you up. I will carry you home if you become exhausted in this journey." He offers walls of safety that create a sanctuary for hope.

Visions of Paradise

Standing within the walls that shelter us, we can still see the gate where worries may enter. But we can also sense the protective stance of the One who guards the gate. The ancient wall is a testament to the faithful protection of the Master Gardener over centuries.

Along the Garden Path

We enter an uneven path, bearing the worn marks of many well-trod days. The psalm bursts from the start with words of relief for the sheer joy of God's goodness awakened in entering this place, "recounting all his wonderful deeds."

The path was once orderly. With time, it has worn, and now we need to be redirected, guided to reach our destination. It is clearly going somewhere majestic.

The psalm propels you, body and soul, forward. Unburdened, you may experience an extraordinary fearlessness. With this unexpected taste of freedom, you may find yourself speaking without restraint. Your constricted heart may start spilling over with words of gratitude, appreciation, and triumph.

You enter this place enabled to recount all that the Giver has gifted you.

Even on this path, you will be aware of the malicious work of others. You suddenly hope for the One who is willing to restore the damage.

Along the way, you pass memorials honoring the memories of the abandoned. Humble and meek, they are forgotten. Except here, at this place of refuge, is a place to remember the vanished who need someone to say, "We know your name." The One who has planted these memorials never forgets us, nor does he forsake his family.

Ahead of us are the gates of this walled refuge. Written on the gate is the name Zion, the place of sanctuary, open for all to enter.

Here is a sheltering place within the garden. Leave your mortal pride at the gate, and as you enter, feel the Breath of God.

Let go of what you have left behind.

Savor the taste of newfound joy.

Indwelling the Garden

Inhale, exhale, feel the desire to be filled; now read.

1 I will give thanks to the Lord with
all my heart;
I will tell of all Your wonders.

Springs delight from deep within
My needs are met in You,
My voice shall sing to tell of all
The marvels that You do.

2 I will rejoice and be jubilant in You;
I will sing praise to Your name,
O Most High.

"Rejoice" shall be my native tongue,
"Thanks" shall be my tune,
Melodies set free shall ring
To You, oh God Triune.

3 When my enemies turn back,
They stumble and perish before You.

Wayward roads lead to the dark
To stumble in the night,
Stalwart in the haze alone,
A vain and fleeting flight.

4 For You have maintained my just cause;
You have sat on the throne judging righteously.

My upward path is clearly lit,
A straight and even way,
You provide, my Healing Helper,
For steady, sustaining days.

5 You have rebuked the nations,
You have eliminated the wicked;
You have wiped out their name forever and ever.

You reprove eroding egos,
Stopping their persistent flood,
Burying the blot of their hurt exposed,
Those pouring out pure blood.

6 The enemy has come to an end *in* everlasting ruins,
And You have uprooted the cities;
The very memory of them has perished.

Their havoc finds a final wall,
Your hand shall still their storm,
Their riot tore the night apart,
But You renew our morn.

7 But the LORD sits *as King* forever;
He has established His throne for judgment.

Crowned with integrity, ever enthroned,
Your realm is the stars and land.
You chart the course of galaxies
And form a baby's hand.

8 And He will judge the world in righteousness;
He will execute judgment for the peoples fairly.

You alone can judge the true
To lead the steady march,
While the nations struggle in hopeless strife,
You bring your peace-pledged arch.

9 The LORD will also be a stronghold for the oppressed,
A stronghold in times of trouble;

Downtrodden souls may rest in calm
Within Your sheltering walls.
Turbulent times shall come and go
Inside love's health-giving halls.

10 And those who know Your name will put their trust in You,
For You, LORD, have not abandoned those who seek You.

Those who know that they are known,
Abandon all to You.
Their journey's shared with Him who cares
And brings serenity's dew.

11 Sing praises to the LORD, who dwells in Zion;
Declare His deeds among the peoples.

Lift high the horn, your voices raise,
For Him who fills the land.
Tell us again the Story new
Of all the joy He's planned.

12 For He who requires blood remembers them;
He does not forget the cry of the needy.

His lifeblood alone may atone,
One takes another's place.
The final peace rests in His hand
To mend all harm through grace.

13 Be gracious to me, LORD;
See my oppression from those who hate me,
You who lift me up from the gates of death,

Pour compassion on my head,
Cleanse me from within,
I'm bruised, confused, and full of strife,
Save me from my sin.

14 So that I may tell of all Your praises,
That in the gates of the daughter of Zion
I may rejoice in Your salvation.

Then I shall sing a morning song
Like snow on gentle land.
Your saving kiss shall touch my lips
As a child held by Your hand.

15 The nations have sunk down into the pit which they have made;
In the net which they hid, their own foot has been caught.

A continental confusion
Of conflicts bred in fear,
Brings disorder and delusion,
Hunters caught in their traps like deer.

16 The LORD has made Himself known;
He has executed judgment.
A wicked one is ensnared in the work of his own hands.
[Selah]

You are unveiled in splendor,
Who set the seas in place.
Renewing order once again
And harmony face to face.
[Again and again, I rest in You]

17 The wicked will return to Sheol,
All the nations who forget God.

From speck we come, to less return,
Without the breath of God,
Significance comes from Him alone,
When deprived, we're fatally flawed.

18 For the needy will not always be forgotten,
Nor the hope of the afflicted perish forever.

No child's too small, no village so lost,
To ever be gone from His sight.
We are anchored, deep in His heart
A harbor through every night.

19 Arise, LORD, do not let mankind prevail;
Let the nations be judged before You.

Reign on, Oh King, Your heartland spare,
Cease all the threatening tides,
May Your table draw all peoples near
To live content at your side.

20 Put them in fear, LORD;
Let the nations know that they are *merely* human.
[Selah]

Reverence, deep as the ocean floor,
Birth in the hearts of all,
To know that You still spin their globe,
And all are loved, though very small.
[We rest in You]

Taking Reflections with You

You are in a sheltered place. Accept that the past has no power over you and feel a calm hope for the future. Let your soul simmer as your attention is engulfed in his presence.

Feel the tension of what is unknown about your future. Now, release your worry and let joy come with an "Oh well; that is not mine to control." Take a quick gasp of gratitude for what you have.

- What *images or words in the psalm* make you feel cared for and important so that you know God more profoundly? What words make you realize what you want him to remember about you?
- How are you coming to see God's role in watching over you, allowing you to understand God in a new way?

- How did this psalm focus on or resonate *with your life*? What is becoming clear regarding *who you are* in the eyes of God and why you need his presence?
- What is becoming more possible in living one day at a time in *your relationship with* God? Think of this as the features of growing confidence and deep, mutual caring.
- What did *he say* to *you* from this psalm that delights you deep within your thoughts and feelings?
- What song or words do you want to sing or say back to him as rejoicing or expressing gratitude?

Final Embrace

Walls may keep you safe from threats until they also keep you from exploration. Read slowly to savor the safety that allows you to live into deepening closeness. Each word is a window to feel beyond the walls and feel hope.

Anticipation.
Jubilation.
Joyful speculation.
Acclaim.
Your Name.
Aerobics.
For the heart.
We have.
Found a meeting place.
Without fear.
Closeness with open space.
Wonder and wasteland.
Spreading wide.
None can hide.
Vanquished or valued?
Who am I in Your grace?
Remembered?
Forgotten?
What is my past's future fate?
It's getting late.
I contemplate.
Your eternity with my vanishing memory.
Who deserves what?
I'll take mercy.
A moment's clarity.
Humble charity.
In case I'm guilty.
Blind to depravity.
Wanting only You to see.
So free.
Some dignity.
Reclaimed.
Realized.
Sheltered.

Psalm 10

Struggling with the Vulnerable in Pursuit of an Undiminished Life

Arise, Lord! Lift up your hand, O God. Do not forget the helpless.
(Psalm 10:12 NIV)

Surveying the Garden

Sometimes, our enemies are strangers; at times, they are neighbors or even nearer yet.

This psalm wrestles with social inequity in our neighborhoods and beyond.

The psalmist inhabits the vulnerability of those who yearn for justice. These are complex issues: We are dealing with matters embedded in our culture and sometimes hidden deeply inside the human heart. As we delve into the psalm, our distant sympathy transforms into a divine empathy. We are driven by a desire to manifest God's love and purpose through meaningful actions.

Even this tender and pleasant garden place is under threat. Intruders terrify you. You want God to defend the Garden from the invasive nuisances that infringe upon its beauty. You sometimes wonder whether the Gardener has abandoned this place.

This psalm also addresses those who have given up on God, thinking God has given up on them.

Some people want independence and don't care about God. They can become lost in their own self-satisfaction or protection.

Today, this psalm invites us to stand with the needy against their oppressors. This is not a call to fight the worldly, the God-rejecters. No, you are simply embracing the weak. It is a prayer asking God to deal with the injustices and imbalances you see. Pray that he might help overcome the plight of the poor and dejected, the trampled and the choked out.

We will also encounter atheists. God resists the lies that unravel these people from the actuality of His love. This psalm shows them besotted with illusion, having lost touch with reality. Their amnesia has left them to believe there is no God. In the vacuum that remains, they are "free to do as they please." They are intoxicated by an empty culture of bragging and greed; lustful desires consume them; their days are spent in search of gratification. Their decaying hearts are blind to God. God's love is unconditional, so we know that it is their alienation and losing touch with reality that is rejected here. God's love never fails, even for atheists.

When encountered personally, God becomes the object of our worship and opens us to a life of love. When God is disregarded, the dignity of neighbors is lost, and the fabric of society unravels.

Jesus wants us to be honest about those with blind spots—to God and to us. Think of those focused on their own self-advancement. They may be family members, our neighbors, or our local public servants. They are obsessed with their status. The Spirit does not want us to become embittered or hard-hearted. He wants us to learn to press through difficult situations with him.

Jesus calls you to look to him as your Protector. You will not abandon anyone; you will become their advocate as he is their Advocate. We first seek God's guidance and then where he leads.

Jesus stands with you, looking at those who appear heartless and despising. You see now that they are blind to what you consider good. He invites you to acknowledge their impact and then release them to him. He says to us, "Give Me the burden of your bruised past; I am making all things well. Stay focused on Me."

Into the Garden with God

Jesus came to a world that did not know him. He loved them anyway.

His whole life was spent walking with the downtrodden and confronting those who abused power. He loved sinners and tax collectors just the same. He gave up on no one. His justice was restorative. He continues to bring hope for a coming day where violence no longer constitutes human relations. It is hard for us to see the subtlety of our rejection and distancing; fear informs the core of our emotional resistance in relationships and builds walls between us and other humans and God. Jesus was fearless.

Paul also honestly looked at humanity's plight. He agonized over how to restore humanity. He was not afraid to side with the outcasts, knowing transformation could only happen in light of God making everything right, not by human effort.

By our own efforts, we are rebellious; thus, in Romans, Paul echoes psalm 10 in recounting the ways the peoples of the earth have forgotten, abused, or usurped the sustaining presence of Jesus as Lord. Paul quotes this struggling psalm:

"THEIR MOUTH IS FULL OF CURSING AND BITTERNESS."
(Romans 3:14 NASB)

Paul knows he is not deaf to the condition of humanity adrift from God.

All this is nothing new to God. He will provide us the safest place—the trust we have in him. In the garden today, we have a place to stand, surrounded by statuary that remembers those who have forgotten God. But we, and they, have an Enduring Companion.

In the early morning shadows of the garden, we see God's light vanquishing the obstacles that hinder an honest way of life.

His light allows the garden to burst with color and life. The orphan and the outcast, the forgotten and the failures, and even those who inflict terror find that God's Justice transforms hearts in this part of the garden.

He invites you to let his inbreaking love call you from your hiding places. He beckons you to come and sit among the memories of your monsters and watch the shadows dissolve.

The traumas of the past and present have become statues of pain. Your heart feels weighed down, needing release. There are no shadows in this part of the garden; light invigorates transformation, as he says, "This is your place of belonging now. I am the Father of the fatherless and the failed fathers. Sit with Me to heal the battles within and without."

Visions of Paradise

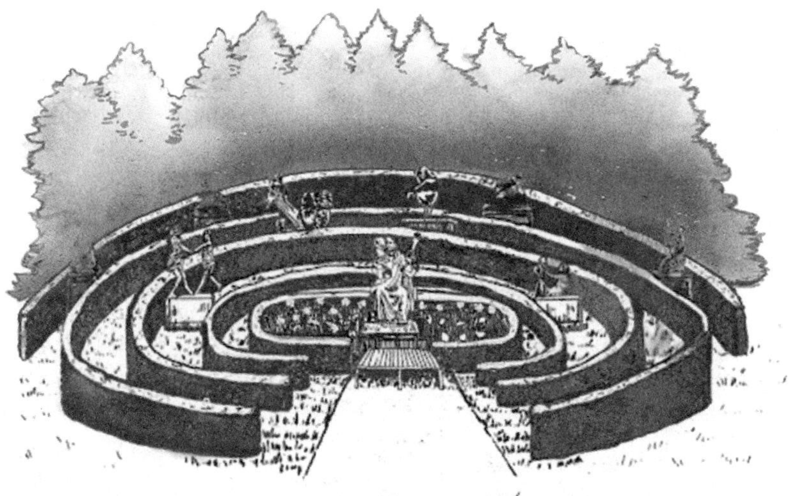

Here, even among the statuary of silent schemers and scoffers, we find peace. We discover that the living are still sustained by the beating heart of the One who cares. He rises to meet the needs of those who require someone to remember them and hear their voice. The stony hearts are silent. The Hearing Heart is here.

Along the Garden Path

On the garden path today, we hear echoes of those who found it inconvenient to acknowledge God. Their soundings haunt the empty spaces intended for love and connection. We feel the weight of their presence.

As you walk this path, past those whose hearts have developed hurtful habits, listen for the Lord of the Lost. He searches for the abandoned, brings wanderers home, and hears with an attentive ear.

Silencing the hard-hearted, the King comes to encourage and establish a comforting estate for us in His garden.

This psalm acknowledges the challenge of living in a world whose deep floods of doubt can submerge us in silence. We may feel an absence. We want our companion on the path. That is why we are here.

Feel the desperate yearning in your heart that longs for God's presence and justice. Let the flame of conviction burn brighter than the darkness of despair and disbelief. You are seeking the One who first sought you.

Indwelling the Garden

Close your eyes for a moment and let the hand in the dark be big enough to hold the world and you. Rest in that palm as you proceed with your eyes open, leaving your desperation in the dark.

1 Why do You stand far away, LORD?
Why do You hide *Yourself* in times of trouble?

Silently, I feel alone,
Where are You, God, tonight?
If You are playing hide-and-seek
I wish You'd come in sight.

2 In arrogance the wicked hotly pursue the needy;
Let them be caught in the plots which they have devised.

I sense the burning pain of stress
From conflicts waged today,
I wish the heartless would meet their match
With a well-placed ricochet.

3 For the wicked boasts of his soul's desire,
And the greedy person curses *and* shows disrespect to the LORD.

Tormentors all, these self-spun beasts
Who thirst for rampant power,
Patting the money-mad on the back,
Whose hearts have long gone sour.

4 The wicked, in his haughtiness, does not seek *Him*.
There is no God in all his schemes.

The compassionless shall wander wide
Missing the steady pole.
His map may reveal where he is,
While excluding the Circling Whole.

5 His ways succeed at all times;
Yet Your judgments are on high, out of his sight;
As for all his enemies, he snorts at them.

Proudly bold, he commands his life,
Disdaining those who resist,
Discarding wisdom from Him who creates,
He slides toward meaninglessness.

6 He says to himself, "I will not be moved;
Throughout the generations I will not be in adversity."

Drunk with delusions,
He spews out self-spun tales.
His safety is all an illusion;
He toasts while his lifeblood fails.

7 His mouth is full of cursing, deceit, and oppression;
Under his tongue is harm and injustice.

His empty words are easily spent,
While oppressing a fellow friend,
That tongue's laced with poison,
Pushing to a deadly end.

8 He sits in the lurking places of the villages;
He kills the innocent in the secret places;
His eyes surreptitiously watch for the unfortunate.

With concealed preparation,
He takes and never gives.
His skills are trained to victimize,
Caring not who dies or lives.

9 He lurks in secret like a lion in his lair;
He lurks to catch the needy;
He catches the needy when he pulls him into his net.

His leering life stalks the streets,
Lurking, as he lures to his lair,
The innocent fall into his clutch,
Snatching at their beauty fair.

10 Then he crushes *the needy one, who* cowers;
And unfortunate people fall by his mighty *power*.

The perching beast prepares to spring,
Catching a fawn unaware,
His sweat is glistening with suspense
Poised for those wandering there.

11 He says to himself, "God has forgotten;
He has hidden His face; He will never see it."

Blind in illusion,
Believing that God's not there,
He's spun a self-made delusion,
"That old God surely won't care."

12 Arise, LORD; God, lift up Your hand.
Do not forget the humble.

Break forth, Defender of all souls,
You, who heal the land,
Remember us in our sorrows;
Raise Your caring hand.

13 Why has the wicked treated God
disrespectfully?
He has said to himself, "You will not
require *an account.*"

Why in the world do you wait to work,
To turn the table around,
Reproving those who laugh in
Your face,
And think they won't be found?

14 You have seen it, for You have
looked at harm and provocation
to take it into Your hand.
The unfortunate commits *himself* to
You;
You have been the helper of the
orphan.

You are not blind to painful loss,
You move against all harm,
You tend to the child who's lost all kin,
Sheltering with boundless charm.

15 Break the arm of the wicked and the
evildoer,
Seek out his wickedness until You
find none.

Constrain the violent, voraciously
vile,
Subvert their driving raid,
Stand secure against their ruin,
Come to our anguished aid.

16 The LORD is King forever and ever;
Nations have perished from His land.

Sovereign King, through halls of
time,
You stand while nations fall,
They're washed away like castle
sand,
Your waves will level all.

17 LORD, You have heard the desire of
the humble;
You will strengthen their heart,
You will make Your ear attentive

With a whispered wail into the
night,
We're seeking for Your ear.
Send a gentle hope-breath back,
Bring peace to fill our years.

18 To vindicate the orphan and
the oppressed,
So that mankind, which is of the
earth, will no longer cause
terror.

Our final fate enfolds in You,
Children not left to chance,
We know You silence injustice,
Bearing the victor's stance.

Taking Reflections with You

Who are you as you prepare to leave the garden? Are you a victim or a victor? It will all depend on who you believe sustains you.

Rest in knowing your true Father is still watching over you and always will.

- What *words* in the psalm awakened past pains and persecutions? What stirred regarding the personal challenge of people who made growing up hard? Are there statues of stone in your heart, the memories of pain that still weigh you down?
- How did God's apparent distance and ongoing involvement hit you as you walked through the psalm? Could you empathize with those who say, "There is no God," or did you want to correct them? What did you see *about God*?
- How did your emotions respond as you dealt with those you thought were friends but abandoned or even harmed you in the past? What is your confidence level in the heart of God as you dust your memories and feel yourself clothed as an embraced child? What did this psalm reveal *about you*?
- What could *your relationship with* God look like if you saw him as living and present, and those who stain your past as statues marking days gone by?
- What words of comfort or restoration can you *hear God address* to you?
- What words of release and acceptance could you *say back*?

Final Embrace

Betrayal can turn into disorientation, shutting us down. The key to going forward is honesty and courage. Consider sharing what you discover later with a trustworthy companion. Try slowly saying what follows out loud.

Why do I feel alone?
I'm wanting.
Wondering.
Waiting.
For You.
Faced.
Full-on.
Abusers.
Defilers.
Heartless.
Faithless.
Fanaticizers.
Blind to beauty.
Void of duty.
Ambushers.
Always snooty.
Tongues.
Tattling.
Travesties.
Lurking.
Smirking.
Winking eyes.
Blackened gaze.
Looking for prey.
Trained.
Stealthy ways.
Remember, remember.
Rise up.
Raise the Justice cup.
Reveal your face.
Don't hesitate.
No internal debate.
Transform our fate.
From vexation.
To restoration.
Thoughtful eyes.
An orphan's reply.
Answered inside.
Hope realized.
You hear.
Heal.
Feel.
Bend Your ear.
Hold my heart.
A start.
From dust.
To delight.
In Your sight.
Reunite.

Psalm 11

Calming with Confidence

The Lord *is in his holy temple; the* Lord *is on*
his heavenly throne.
He observes everyone on earth; his eyes examine them.
(Psalm 11:4 NIV)

Surveying the Garden

Does the thought of God watching you make you feel afraid or comforted?

Fight and flight are two responses to threatening circumstances. Confidence in God is another possibility: learning to turn to face him without fear.

You are entering a psalm charged with challenging, fear-creating voices. You will have several forceful encounters that may affect you existentially. Some voices in life, possibly those of *friends*, trigger the psalmist (and you) to want to escape certain threats, with a call to "look out for yourself." This is flight, running from danger. This is the inner and understandable urge to withdraw for self-preservation.

Also, there is the threat of *attackers*. They may use any means—weapons or words—to tear at our very being. In response, we may distance ourselves from public view—go incognito. This, too, is a form of flight. After some respite, the calm we experience turns out to be illusory. We can only stand the agony for so long. We must fight.

The *world* of this psalm, and maybe our world too, can appear to be falling apart, whether we choose to fight or evade others in our milieu. This can be frightening. When we realize that fear has become a constant motive, we begin to understand why we act like survivalists (flight) or competitors (fight). We are living a reactive, insecure life. We need the solace of the Psalms to deal with our realities.

Many people lead a static, silent existence, immobilized by unrecognized trauma. We try to call this reclusive space "holy" since holy can mean to separate. It is not holy; it is a step into the grave. Our need for solitude gives us a false sense of security. True holiness involves a connection to the One we are set apart to be with. We choose to strike free from distractions to find deeper intimacy with him.

True holiness is separating from our individualized, privatized lives to *be with* God. Our motive is to love God, our neighbor, and whatever else needs our loving attention. We even learn to love ourselves as we have been loved. That place of attentiveness is where this psalm will take us.

Our adventure in the garden now begins. There is no room for a solitary fear-based reaction to the perils we encounter. In fact, the psalmist is aware of the threats ahead. He rejects these and turns to God, thereby taking our attention with him. We are turned to trusting God, who provides the most profound foundation for a life built on love.

Through its patient rhythm, the flow of this psalm steers our attention from unsettling distractions to a calm place centered on the Living God.

This psalm acknowledges that life is full of interruptions. When there is an earthquake, you take cover. Relationships, like earthquakes, can experience seismic upheavals.

Healing comes in remembering *whose* you are. Find refuge today from toxicity—whether personal or mass media-induced—and lift your eyes to see Jesus. He is seated and settled, inviting you to sit with him.

Jesus says, "Let me abide in you. I will not only fill you with peace, but you may also abide in Me to find a place of refuge. My peace is not circumstantial, achieved by controlling every situation. My peace is the fruit of My presence. Relax into Me and allow that release to shed your anxiety and reactivity. Come now, and rest in Me."

Into the Garden with God

Many people miss the value of walking with Jesus. They do not want to make him a priority because they know little about him. They get disoriented and resist, rejecting him or keeping him at an arm's length (or mind's length) away. They fear they will lose something instead of gain if they listen to him.

Even Jesus had to re-center his disciples, who would regularly turn away to meet their own needs. He asked a simple question to see if their hearts had found confidence in him:

> He [Jesus] was asking His disciples, "Who do people say that the
> Son of Man is?" 14 And they said, "Some *say* John the Baptist; and
> others, Elijah; and *still* others, Jeremiah, or one of the *other*
> prophets." 15 He said to them, "But who do you yourselves say
> that I am?" 16 Simon Peter answered, "You are the Christ, the Son
> of the living God."
> (Matthew 16:13–16 NASB)

Breaking through the fear of being wrong, Peter found release in the truth of acknowledging who he is. This awakening to love caused Jesus to change Peter's name and tell him he would build his church on this holy connectedness.

Peter got it—we find confidence in his confidence. He knew who Jesus was. He had confidence that he was with God in the flesh. This is acceptance—the place beyond fear and living embraced. But Peter was tested and sometimes lost confidence.

Peter, soon after, denied Jesus three times under threat. But Jesus knew his heart. Jesus saw into Peter and valued him as a foundational rock upon which to build his church. That was confidence returned by Jesus. There was a secure relationship despite human imperfection. The goal of this psalm is to embrace reality found beyond fear, safe in the grip of grace.

Jesus asks you now, "Who do you say I am, and in whom is your deepest confidence?" This is not a test. It is an opportunity to be free in honesty. Knowing he loves you, whatever the answer, is a breath of freedom. For this moment, he asks you to shed the urge to go anywhere but to be with him. Settle in with him.

Visions of Paradise

This is a love seat intended for sharing. It is not a chair to sit in alone and contemplate. Come and sit awhile. Be re-centered on this One who holds the world, all changing influences of cultures, and your shifting life—now, settle in by his side.

Along the Garden Path

The path of this psalm stretches ahead through a gauntlet of unceasing conflict. We will explore where you put your confidence.

You are on a challenge-course that reveals your vulnerability, living in the gap between trusting God or choosing your favorite escape or distraction. You are loved either way, but that is not what your fears tell you.

Anxiety disorders come into play when we let the little voice inside our head start our worrying. It sounds like caution—"be careful now"—but it is self-concern, putting up defensive walls. The ultimate forms of fear bring complete self-focus. Deep fear is when we withdraw exclusively into ourselves. Confidence in anyone else disappears; we are alone and anxious.

We quickly forget what it means to be courageous or vulnerable on behalf of others. In this psalm, we are about to discover the boldness that comes from knowing we are not alone. This psalm calls for a courageous commitment to trust in God. You are invited to discover the calm that comes from being refocused on the One who sees and knows you.

Everyone is invited to "share" a meal with Jesus. For some, it is a feast of joy and communion. For others, it is a cup of *wrath*. However, we have to take a deeper look at that word.

Wrath is not an "out-of-control emotion" unleashed by an angry God intent on destroying. Like wreaths, which are twisted grapevines, and wraiths, which, for Tolkien, are twisted humans, wrath deals with what is twisted.[2] But the God we know is love; God's wrath untwists a twisted world. God is not twisted. He is dealing with our twistedness and setting everything straight. In love, he says no to abuse, violence, and oppression.

To those being untwisted, this unraveling is painful. God is refining, and it feels stormy and scorching. Love confronts those who cause harm and does what love always desires—setting a restorative course for those who have grieved us. Wrath is not destruction; it is love's obstruction of damaging actions.

Psalm 11 is not experienced in the same way by all. Those who find comfort in God will find it a reassuring stroll. Those who resist God find it confrontive, concerned that correction lies ahead. The intent of the psalm is connection, wherever you may begin.

Ultimately, we are invited to gaze into God's loving eyes. We may yield to the embrace waiting for us as we see his face and feel his heart. He wants to lead us to a state of lasting contentment that truly satisfies our hearts.

Share the confident love with which you resonate, enfolded in his loving intent, and relax into his peace.

---

[2] Tom Shippey, *J.R.R. Tolkien: Author of the Century* (Houghton Mifflin, 2000), 122. This page discussed the connection, which is significant for our understanding of wrath as twistedness. Wrath, as we see in the rest of the Psalms, is God's act of untwisting the twisted.

Indwelling the Garden

Seek, and you will find the One waiting for you. He dwells in heaven but also promises to be with you—you may always find refuge in him.

1 In the LORD I take refuge;
How can you say to my soul, "Flee *as a* bird to your mountain?

I'm seeking sanctuary,
In the forest of Your trust.
I will not flee, as some suggest,
Winging from this world gone bust.

2 For, behold, the wicked bend the bow,
They have set their arrow on the string
To shoot in darkness at the upright in heart.

Will I hide from arrows
Searching for my heart?
I can sense the archer,
Waiting in the dark.

3 If the foundations are destroyed,
What can the righteous do?"

Devastation fills my habitat,
My world has gone awry.
Where, my soul, shall I retreat?
To You, my Guard, I fly.

4 The LORD is in His holy temple;
the LORD's throne is in heaven;
His eyes see, His eyelids test the sons of mankind.

Scanning from Your holy hill,
Your regency supreme,
Your eyes perceive all mortal souls,
You test our life's bloodstream.

5 The LORD tests the righteous and the wicked,
And His soul hates one who loves violence.

You ascertain the threatening foes.
And likewise, find the firm.
You separate the predator,
To quarantine the germ.

6 He will rain coals of fire upon the wicked,
And brimstone and burning wind will be the portion of their cup.

The cancerous threat You will reject,
You purge the death-seed's grip.
Complete in restoration,
Ending the plague's cruel script.

[7] For the LORD is righteous, He
loves righteousness;
The upright will see His face.

Ten thousand days of bright-lit
love
Embrace me with Your care.
You grant to gaze into Your eyes
While Your fingers bring
repair.

Confidence comes from a history of promise and fulfillment. The Father, who created the world, sent Jesus, poured out the Holy Spirit, and knows your every hair, has promised he will never forget or abandon you. Rest in him.

Taking Reflections with You

You have breathed in the breath of confidence. Exhale all the fear that triggers the impulse to flee or hide. Breathe in again the faithful presence of Jesus. Confidence is a way of being with another person that transforms us because we now know what faithful care feels like. Let his presence do the transforming.

- What sensations triggered you as you read over *the words* of this psalm? Did you discover that you have trust issues?
- How did God show up for you in this reading? Could you find confidence in God in a calming way?
- What did this psalm bring to the surface from the hidden places of your life? How do you deal with digging up buried issues to find secure feelings? What is becoming apparent about *who you are in all this*?
- What would be possible today in *your relationship with* God if you could find confidence in him? How could a growing relationship with him help in the uncomfortable situations you face today?
- Hear the Spirit, coming as the Comforter, speaking to your situations with words intended for you alone.
- Let God's healing fingers release your lips, opening them and releasing what is twisted inside. Let your words in response to him be an opening for the unsettledness inside to be spoken and unleashed to be untwisted.

Final Embrace

God's presence allows us to be free from fear controlling our lives. When fear is gone, proper playfulness and connection are released in us as symptoms of our restoration to freedom. Speak freedom in your heart as you read.

Priority.
You next to me.
Confidently.
How could it not be?
Those alarmists.
Focused on harming.
Unnerving.
Calling for fleeing.
Flit and flutter.
Run for cover.
Retreating.
Sweat beading.
Bolting.
Dodging.
Evading.
While foundations crumble.
Society sliding.
Truths colliding.
Excuses presiding.
Violence reigning.
Disintegration swaying.
But look.
Eyes everseeing.
With us, He's freeing.
Watching.
Searching.
Eyelids wide.
Hearts seen inside.
Resisting havoc.
A grace-filled fanatic.
Detesting violence.
Bringing love's opulence.
A chalice of allegiance.
Refining.
Redefining.
Sharing.
Repairing.
Racing to grace.
Met face-to-face.
Delighting gaze.
Remembered.
Respecting.
Assured.
Heard.
Confident.

Psalm 12

The Predicament and Possibility of Listening

And the words of the Lord *are flawless,*
like silver purified in a crucible, like gold refined seven times.
(Psalm 12:6 NIV)

Surveying the Garden

To flourish, gardens demand weeding and watering. To communicate effectively, our speech must be clear and connected. God consistently weeds out the unnecessary in our lives and speaks to illuminate our understanding.

Weeding out our conversations involves filtering out propaganda, polluting words, and the misunderstandings that bombard us.

This psalm exposes the predicaments we face each day. We are shaped by what and who we listen to. We may feel socially saturated by various media voices that incite fear and prey on our powerlessness. Part of what we hear may be accurate, but distortions create worry and confusion.

So much of what confronts us has a hidden agenda. There's a common tendency for people to showcase their strengths and virtues while vilifying their opponents. Sorting out the truth can be bewildering. Who will we ever trust? Those seeking power often distort the truth; honesty is sacrificed, and principles are abandoned; their words betray the trust inherent in faithful relationships. All in the drive for victory.

Amid this troubling situation, the voice of God speaks with clarity and faithfulness. What does God promise? His faithful presence, unconditional love for the unloved, rescue for the oppressed, and resistance to the corrupt.

God's words are like gold, clearing the air of confusion. Jesus, the Word made flesh, is our Living Water. He faithfully sustains us with God's love, bringing enjoyment to our lives as the fruit of his presence.

The Gardener shows up today, speaking words of promise: "I will do something for you today. I will be with you in your suffering, discouragement, and sense of overwhelm. I am with you, not silently, but as the One who never tires of saying, 'I will be with you always.'"

Into the Garden with God

The task of the Living God is to give us a true and faithful promise. He tells us who he is and what he is committed to. He is the One who holds the universe and our lives together. He calls us to keep focused on his involvement in our lives.

Competing voices fill our gardens. Like invasive weeds, they infringe on our ability to hear the Word of God. They whisper into our ears and try to change our minds. We can be restored by the One who is the true source of our vitality.

In the Letter to the Romans, Paul deals with divisions confronting the young congregation in Rome by redirecting them—and us—to Christ, the One who is our Meeting Place with God. In Christ, we know we are secure as beloved children because we are encircled by God, who is for us and with us.

In the face of opponents' bitter accusation, personal affront, and physical altercation, Paul leads us to clarity, found in the True Word of God:

> What then shall we say to these things? If God *is* for us,
> who *is* against us?
> (Romans 8:31 NASB)

God speaks reality into being and keeps communicating his sustaining presence. We are learning to hear the faithful voice of God. His loving affirmations ward off all complaint, blame, accusation, and heavy silence. Like shadows, his light dispels their lies.

God's purifying presence cleanses your contaminated mind. He is for you. Nothing can stand against you. Hear his voice, discard every frivolous word.

Come to the grotto in the garden, a place set aside to listen and focus on the words of God. They speak of his heart of gold. His words are refined like a precious metal, strong, and trustworthy. He says, "I am gracious, compassionate, patient, abounding in lovingkindness, and forgiving. Listen and look at Me; let Me clean your soul."

Visions of Paradise

A grotto is a sanctuary for listening and focusing. Its retreat sensibility clears a space to hear healing words. Here, you will find security in a focused invitation to contemplate the words gracious, compassionate, patient, abounding in lovingkindness, *and* forgiving, *unveiling his heart for you.*

Along the Garden Path

Sometimes, we must learn to listen to find our way along the path.

A sound ahead may lead you or deceive you. This psalm alerts us to the voices that might divert us from our goal. The path we seek guides us toward compassionate and loving hope.

This path opens with a plea and a memory of a time when we were fortunate to have faithful companions who committed time and energy to listening and responding to us. They were loyal, dependable, honest people who almost felt like family—maybe they were family.

But those faithful friends seem to have faded away. Death takes its toll; some move away. More become unavailable, consumed elsewhere, while others sever ties without explanation. Our worlds tilt as the people move around us.

In this psalm, the focus is on people who have become untrustworthy, and their feelings of insecurity are evident. Something is amiss. They are absent or withholding part of the story. They silence the truth, crafting falsehoods to keep us apart.

Lies are so compelling and dangerous precisely because people are generally unaware of others' deceptions. We remain blissfully ignorant—until the truth shatters our perception.

Those who offer friendship but never have time or energy for it are often revealed to be seeking affirmation, rather than authentic connection. They are often lonely people, quick to people please, but their inner life is contrary to all you see—it is a counterfeit friendship.

More dreadfully, this psalm leads you to walk past those who have traumatized you in the past, triggering your emotions, an ambush that becomes a fresh attack. Their words pierce your serenity. Words fly like shrapnel, sometimes with surgical stealth. They drain your lifeblood, flooding you with bad memories, the voices of old critics returning to haunt.

These people find fulfillment in wielding power, scorning God or any authority beyond their own desires. Their tongue is their chisel. They sculpt the world according to their own narcissistic vision. You are nothing more than an obstacle to be cleared for their ambition.

In the midst of it all, a light breaks through. The exploiters' deceit is exposed. The cries of hidden souls are addressed.

"I will do something here," Jesus says. He will meet our broken selves with grace, compassion, patience, lovingkindness, and forgiveness. He is the caretaker of this garden, providing the foundation for growth and tending it with love. He reminds us that His garden was made to be filled with warmth, lightness, and revitalization.

Jesus's words ring true.

Now, the Gardener is done weeding the soil. He has acted against the indecent and their empty promises. The garden glows with safety and security. Peace at last; we have peace at last.

The grotto of serene listening is before you. Enter to know its healing presence.

Indwelling the Garden

Pay attention to your ears and how they connect to your heart. See these receptors as unguarded openings, leaving you vulnerable. Jesus will enter this place with you. He will restore your listening today and give your heart space to expand.

1 Help, LORD, for the godly person
has come to an end,
For the faithful have disappeared
from the sons of mankind.

2 They speak lies to one another;
They speak with flattering lips and
a double heart.

3 May the LORD cut off all flattering
lips,
The tongue that speaks great
things;

4 Who have said, "With our tongue
we will prevail;
Our lips are our own; who is lord
over us?"

5 "Because of the devastation of the
poor, because of the groaning of
the needy,
Now I will arise," says the LORD;
"I will put him in the safety for
which he longs."

6 The words of the LORD are pure
words;
Like silver refined in a furnace on
the ground, filtered seven times.

7 You, LORD, will keep them;
You will protect him from this
generation forever.

Aid me in my time of need,
I live in huddled fear,
Resounding voices fade away
Of those who love You dear.

Flying words, like windblown weeds,
Swirling fills the air.
Across the fields, flattery flows,
With a vain, fraudulent flair.

Cease the tides of lyrical lies,
Masked in melody mild.
Like a murky fountain snorting out mud,
Spewing words now gone wild.

Flung out commands to grip the heart
Say, "We are in control,"
Their self-success, a fleeting mirage,
Now appear as a sunken hole.

The weary weak give a painful shriek,
The earth bows as the Master stands,
"Your ache for peace will now be met
In the palms of My outstretched
hands."

A resurrected spring of flowing words
Means winter's death is done,
Refined from gold, bringing liquid
truth,
Glory's speech has finally sprung.

LORD, secure these sapling souls,
Who fear the drift of time.
Grow our family strong and sure,
Hung with love's beckoning chimes.

[8] The wicked strut about on every
side
When vileness is exalted among the
sons of mankind.

Dispel the roosters, who spoil the
scene,
Invading from every edge.
They salute a statue of selfish
pride,
Toasting their hollow pledge.

The words of God are wisdom for the mind and healing for the heart. Let the Spirit bring the cleansing heart of God to exhume all your dead thoughts and voices. Then, let the Spirit replant to make fresh places in your heart, filled with the light, love, and seeds of good fruit.

Taking Reflections with You

Finally, you are sitting at a listening point. Pay attention to the inner dialogue that emerges when you're overwhelmed and think, "Oh God, I need somebody!" This psalm is a cry for help. It is also a promise of help.

- What *words* in this psalm engage the voices that you have in your past and present, and leave scars or fading tattoos? What words still cut, and what ones speak of your dignity and value?
- How did God's speaking make who God is more present? In what way did you find the words of God helped you *hear* God, creating a new way that reveals who he is?
- How did this psalm open your ears to *hear yourself*? What did you discover about how others' words have shaped how you understand *who you are*?
- How does listening to this psalm impact your view of your *relationship* with God?
- What authentic words do *you hear* Jesus, his Father, or the Holy Spirit say to you?
- What is the most authentic thing you can *say back* to God?

Final Embrace

Sometimes, it rains cleansing tears to hide your own. Sometimes, the sun sneaks up on you and makes rainbows. We live with changing emotional weather and need resilience to weather the storms. Let it rain.

Agendas.
Vendettas.
Umbrella for defenses.
Scanning.
Planning.
Fawning.
Flattering.
Inward decaying.
Friends vanishing.
Good folk disappearing.
Alone.
Abandoned.
Crying.
Dying.
People lying.
Shells of neighbors.
Babbling on.
Hearts gone.
Doomed to con.
Vain mates.
Falsehood irritates.
Empty inside.
Truth denied.
Tongue trips.
Lost in the counterfeits.
Sharpening the words.
Control seems absurd.
Thundering . . . until we heard,
"I am ready.
Always steady.
Nothing too petty.
I speak.
Rescuing the weak.
Acting to critique.
Although My heart is meek.
My love is so unique."
Crucible.
Purifying syllables.
Heart flows with a mouth full.
Gold for real.
Into your depths.
Taking those first steps.
From needy to plenty.
Shedding triviality.
Sitting on Your knee.
Love raining down on me.
Soaked.
Cloaked.
Stoked.
Fear revoked.
Words.
Reverberating.
Harmony.

Psalm 13

Abandonment and Adoration

"How long, LORD? Will you forget me forever?
How long will you hide your face from me?"
(Psalm 13:1 NIV)

Surveying the Garden

This psalm pursues a deep quest. It grapples with our sense of God's absence, which could raise a question of God's abandonment of us or our inattentiveness to him.

This psalm's questioning is not just about knowing God, but about finding a restored sense of God's presence. That is the quest for intimacy in the Psalms. Silence can easily be misread, but he is there.

These passages resonate with people like Job, the author of Ecclesiastes, and the countless pilgrims, like you, who want to know God as present and living. The shared experience of humanity wrestles with a sense of absence, especially in the midst of pain and doubt.

With the void comes distress, anxiety, depression, loneliness, and sometimes deep despair or agony. Today, the garden echoes with emptiness and prayers of urgency. The deep yearning for intimacy permeates every fiber of our being. This hunger cuts to the core of our existence as persons.

The whole of our being is at stake in this psalm. We are facing who we are and will become in life's challenging pilgrimage. Our body will face the threat of aging and eventually death. Our emotions are often spent in sorrow or weariness. Our thinking is often interrupted, consumed by questions that entomb us.

Who are you in "moments of missing" like a "minus one," in a romantic setting, feeling all alone? You cannot be the same "you" when a beloved other is absent. You want to go through life as a "plus one." Even those who are single need family and friends to maintain emotional health. You need others in order to fully be you, especially as your anchor in the storm. Hope remains but diminishes as you are worn down.

Abandonment issues often arise from unfulfilled expectations. These may occur due to prolonged absences or becoming aware that the care of another is lacking. What is missing is feeling valued. This may manifest as feeling forgotten, perhaps devalued, or missing the assurance that you matter. It sucks the life out of you. Being valued and belonging give us the gift of being found desirable. Our life has meaning. That is what God's love establishes for you.

This void echoes with your absence, a longing for reunion.

This psalm reveals that even in life's most confusing moments, we find God's unwavering faithfulness. He knows you and says, "They are singing our song," and you know you have found the One who resonates with your soul.

Seated at his table, with bread and wine of remembering, you recall this One as a faithful friend. He is not lost in the past; he has always been there for you. He is present as he remembers you to himself. Presence comes in the remembering of feeling at ease and at home.

Upon returning to his table and eating with him, you recognize that his absence reminded you that you desire him, and he is fond of you returning regularly. Absence was anticipation.

The sun comes out. You feel like celebrating. You now experience the happiness that overcomes feelings of neglect caused by your misplaced focus.

Jesus's presence brings an attitude adjustment. He has been patient, waiting for your return. He dances over the void and invites you to join him.

Jesus says, "I have you. I always do. Breathe in My readiness to stand by you, walk with you, and carry you through. Then sing out that song of gladness. Let our song expand in you with all the passion and joy that can be exhaled from you. Let My Spirit renew you, wash your pain, and bring you into the pleasure of Our company. You are not alone."

Into the Garden with God

The psalmist acknowledges but is also concerned by our profound longing for connection. This longing is not a bad thing. It echoes a spoken love, shared in the past, still yearning for reunion.

Yearning for the face of the one you love reveals your heart's orientation. When they are gone, your face loses its glow, and the light in your eyes dims.

This psalm illuminates our core commitment, allowing us to feel our pulse rise as we seek to find this kind of love that hungers for face-to-face connection.

This desire to see the face of God is portrayed in the Aaronic blessing:

The LORD bless you, and keep you;
25 the LORD cause His face to shine on you, and be gracious to you;
26 the LORD lift up His face to you, and give you peace.
(Numbers 6:24–26 NASB)

This is a prayer with a goal of a transforming gaze. When the Lord turns toward us, we bask in the warmth of his shining face. This personal connection, initiated by Jesus and reflected in our faces, continues to have an impact until his grace finally reaches our hearts.

In 1 Corinthians, being face-to-face with God is anticipated as our ultimate goal. For now, God is mediated in a reflected way, like seeing someone standing behind you glimpsed in a mirror. In the mirror, you may catch an echoed image of them; you have to turn around to look at them face-to-face.

This reflection of God points us to reality. It awakens a desire for deep togetherness. Paul says,

For now we see only a reflection as in a mirror;
then we shall see face to face. Now I know in part;
then I shall know fully, even as I am fully known.
(1 Corinthians 13:12 NIV)

Knowing and being known is the final bliss.

Today, we are like-minded with Paul, intent on the time when face-to-face encounters achieve the fullness of love and joy. We live with the current reality and acknowledge the emerging sense of distance.

Jesus sees you on the other side of the maze of life. He promises, "I am here. Talk to me. Eat my Meal. Be with those who love Me. My life is the shared life; share it with Me."

Visions of Paradise

A maze is full of anticipation and waiting to reach the far end. How long one will be in the maze depends on how well one knows the way, or desires to get to someone waiting at the other end. It is full of mystery, but the anxiety of the journey is worth it for the reconnection at the finish.

Along the Garden Path

"How much longer?" is a typical back-seat complaint. A child's anxiety reveals that they have not yet learned to enjoy the journey. But it is an honest question that needs an answer.

Telling a story about the joy of seeing the person at the destination can refocus on hope, creating a picture of being met with a smile, a hug, and a good laugh.

This path we are on today is not easy. It is a long pilgrimage. It begins with being perplexed.

The psalmist is stuck between memories of connection and delight with his God, as well as the impending, threatening possibility of death. Enemies lurk near the psalmist; they will be glad when he is gone; their jeers are in his ears.

This is a grief observed, life out of control. Ahead is the slog of daily endurance.

Four times the words echo out on the "Welcome Mat" of this psalm: "How long?" There is a tense feeling that, if this is a game of hide-and-seek, it has been too long! This is an intensely personal path. Fear floods one's thoughts. Is this rejection? Is this absence or simply neglect? Whatever it is, it tears at the heart. *How long?*

His thoughts, a tangled maze, present a bewildering series of considerations. Reflecting on these feelings is an isolating experience. Plans and possibilities that were a cause for joy have now become a racket inside our heads.

During the storm, you are covered with a blanket of grief. You wish you could just hide, to be left alone. It is made worse by a further hailstorm of agitators that batter and ridicule you.

Finally, your anxiety begs for intervention. You want to be heard. You need answers. You want to be seen.

The darkness of death dissolves as you awaken to heaven's breaking light. Now, there is a glow in your eye, not coming from within; it reflects his light. The Spirit has found you and brought you to the welcoming presence of God. You feel courageous.

Then, an awareness of God's unfailing love comes to you. The rain and sunshine of emotions all come at once. The cleansing rays of hope create a rainbow, a reminder of God's covenant love. Suddenly, you are sustained by trust. Your heart enlarges. The storm clouds are swept away.

Then comes the song. The melody is simple and sweet, sung from long ago. It is the melody of divine hope.

You realize that the feeling of unrequited love was simply a result of your forgetfulness. God's love comes to us first and is unconditional. That love never fails. What remains is our response: to be free, made whole by the One who loved us all along. Belonging is the final resolve.

This is the spring that we drink from; this is the source of our exuberance. The song inside breaks into expressions of simple desire, to bask in the generous goodness of this One who is our resounding joy.

Much of our life is anticipation. But stay on the path and feel the sacred touch of unreserved grace and healing at the end. Take the step, knowing it is an adventure together.

Indwelling the Garden

[1]How long, LORD? Will you forget me forever?
How long will you hide Your face from me?

Never-ending wait,
You seem so late,
As I linger in this silent time.
When will Your face
Make present your grace?
On Your lap I long to climb.

[2]How long am I to feel anxious in my soul,
With grief in my heart all the day?
How long will my enemy be exalted over me?

My musing mind
Confusion finds
I need Your calming voice.
I feel within
A saddening spin
As foes infringe my choice.

[3]Consider *and* answer me, O LORD my God;
Enlighten my eyes, or I will sleep the *sleep of* death,

Respond and see,
Oh, LORD who frees,
Illuminate my sight.
My heart grows dim
I fade within;
Death is my steady plight.

[4]And my enemy will say, "I have overcome him,"
And my adversaries will rejoice when I am shaken.

I feel put down,
In tears I drown,
Enduring hurtful acts.
Adversity hails,
My spirit fails;
Enemies laugh at my lack.

[5]But I have trusted in Your faithfulness;
My heart shall rejoice in Your salvation.

I bathe in Your love,
Poured from above,
Your compassion never fails.
My ecstasy swells,
Your joy indwells,
Now safe from all that ails.

6 I will sing to the LORD,
Because He has looked after me.

My voice shall dance,
My feet shall prance,
Abundance shall fill my life.
Your daily gifts
Shall heal all rifts;
Your provisions heal all strife.

Taking Reflections with You

You have probably known dark places of disappointment. Today you have an appointment to meet with the One who is always available—the appointment is *for us* to take time, not because he is hard to get in to see!

- Do any *words* in this psalm resonate with your sense of God not being available for you? What *words awaken* in you the enduring faithfulness of God?
- How did this psalm awaken your desire to cry out, "How long?" In what way did the movement that began with desperation and ends in exaltation help you to see the nature of God in your life in a new way?
- How did this psalm center you regarding what is missing and what your ultimate joy is in fulfilling *who you are*? What is your identity in relation to suffering? Do you feel a victim in any way?
- What does this psalm reveal about *your relationship with* God? To whom or what do you give your whole heart and being? What does it feel like to awaken to One who affirms his never-ending love?
- When his love breaks through in this psalm, what do you hear *spoken to you*?
- What *words of response* would you mirror back to God from this psalm?

Final Embrace

Sitting in a cloud of unknowing, we feel an internal push in our waiting with big questions, wanting big answers. Questions are the keys to life that take us beyond the clouds to see what is known there. Life is best if we let discovery be our guide. Read and see what you discover in each word as a window to your emotions.

Impatient.
Forgotten.
Waiting.
Debating.
Where are You?
This lonely view.
Feeling tossed.
Lost.
If only.
You were here too.
Without You.
Distress.
Within me.
Sorrow.
Above me.
Silence.
Around me.
Intimidation.
Wrestling.
Perplexing.
Grieved.
Bereaved.
Needing You beside.
Intervene.
Look at me!
Listen to me. . . .
Shine on me.
Ignite in me.
The fire of You.
Renew.
Infuse.
Love profuse.
Heartened news.
Your promise true.
I sense the warmth.
The joy.
The trust.
Your evermust.
To stand.
Sustain.
Be the same.
I know.
I know.
I know.
You are there.
Wellspring.
Life to bring.
Joy.
Release.
Peace.
Songs to free.
In me.
Adoration.

Psalm 14

Living with Void or Vitality

The Lord looks down from heaven on all mankind
to see if there are any who understand,
any who seek God.
(Psalm 14:2 NIV)

Surveying the Garden

Perspective matters. *Who* you stand with matters just as much as *where* you stand.

Today we will view the garden from a balcony—with God. Seeing the bigger picture of what is unfolding below, we gain insight into the impact of missing or avoiding God's way of life.

Standing with God, we are given telephoto lenses to see into the secrets of people's hearts. Some simply refuse to acknowledge God. Others become godly-wise because they learn to listen and follow.

Tragically, those in denial often miss vital life insights. Self-interest corrupts their choices. With hardened hearts, they become blind to the way of love. They become foolish, and friendships fade away. They become like summer weeds, lacking secure roots and enduring beauty. They consume and have forgotten how to contribute.

But consider the wise person, memorialized in the abundance of a fruit tree or a flowering bush, that awakens memories of all the tender care they embody. They drink deeply of the waters of lovingkindness and become other-centered. They allow God's gifts to overflow into caring actions. They love to share. Their hearts have nothing to hide or deny.

Love's wisdom is clear when contrasted with that of those who are entirely self-focused. The heart at work becomes evident in the outcome of each person's actions. We stand with Jesus to learn how to distinguish the wise from the foolish. What is "wise to the world" may be unwise in light of the grace of God.

Jesus invites you to stand with him, but he does not want you to become judgmental. He wants healing for the bullies and for those who are oblivious to stop their damaging actions. He wants to encourage the trampled so they will not lose heart.

Jesus beckons to you, saying, "Look with wise eyes and see the loss in life of those who will not accept My love. Notice how different they are from those who taste my joy embedded within them. Become wise as you watch them with Me. They all need our love."

Into the Garden with God

This challenging psalm is about learning to see differences.

It is easy to scan the fields of humanity across the world and assume they are all basically the same. What we cannot chart is the long-range impact of being without God.

Spiritually impoverished individuals are struggling to survive in a competitive world. The urge for survival forms a self-focused heart. Their hearts narrow to see from a limited perspective; they miss what you discover when you stand with Jesus—seeing the world he loves and the tragic consequences of turning away from him.

But is anyone on earth *not* burdened with the spiritual blindness that misses God?

All have sinned. All have lost their bearings. Separated from God, they are unaware of their decline until it is too late. Then, there is violence everywhere—like at the time of the great flood.

Human hospitality and generosity can sadly deteriorate and become predatory, feeding exploitatively on one another. Others are to be exploited, to be taken advantage of to satisfy one's own desires. This psalm explodes with these images.

This revelation is why Paul uses this psalm in the Letter to the Romans. He pulls back the curtain on the naked truth. He exposes a world that has forgotten, denied, or lost all knowledge of God's presence:

> [10] As it is written:
> "THERE IS NO RIGHTEOUS PERSON, NOT EVEN ONE;
> [11] THERE IS NO ONE WHO UNDERSTANDS,
> THERE IS NO ONE WHO SEEKS OUT GOD;
> [12] THEY HAVE ALL TURNED ASIDE,
> TOGETHER THEY HAVE BECOME CORRUPT;
> THERE IS NO ONE WHO DOES GOOD,
> THERE IS NOT EVEN ONE."
> (Romans 3:10–12 NASB)

This is truth-telling. Without the grace through God's self-revealing to us, we share the inclination of humanity to seek our interests in more or less self-serving lifestyles. We are made new only because of him, not by our effort or achievement. All is grace.

This is not a psalm that condemns or provides comfort, nor does it side with the oppressed or oppressors. It is a call to return to God and get real. Some people may see us as "religious people who have lost touch with reality." But this psalm establishes reality in the One who comes from Zion, the meeting place of God. His reality comes to restore and renew the joy for which he created the world.

Jesus spreads a table with bread and wine on the balcony. He invites you to come and survey the desperate situation in the world. Rather than looking with despair, he tells you, "I have it all under My care. I know how to dance on the void and chaos and bring resurrection hope." Breathe out a sigh of relief to release the anxiety.

Visions of Paradise

This balcony is a place of observation, offering a panoramic view of all that lies below. As you stand here with Jesus, think of his heart being developed in you. He wants you to learn to discern the spectrum of human states. He wants you to see with kind eyes those devoid of or delighting in God's goodness—and to have a heart of compassion, grace, and mercy. Then, you can be a source of hope for all and share Jesus's heart, never giving up on anyone—because Jesus does not.

Along the Garden Path

Who is normal? Outside, people appear similar enough to us to believe there are some common standards. Beyond the veil of their humanity, as bodies before us, are worlds of difference.

Many, if not most, people are calloused to your presence and to Jesus. They have little consciousness of anyone else but themselves. Many people may *not* say, "There is no God," but you *may hear* them mutter,

"Leave me alone." That is their reality. Something has died inside them. Their hearts are disconnected from the field of persons surrounding their hollow, medicated lives. Their sense of belonging probably matches the emptiness of their sadly isolated heart.

Those who reject God's guidance often spread despair and cynicism to others. Their scorn can be contagious. They persecute the happy and hopeful. It is a tragic unraveling.

The psalm you are about to enter brings you to the bad edge of human experience. You will encounter the defection from God, which is the actual state of the world.

Considering how dire the situation is, and seeing what God sees, you realize that few are looking up. Many are trying to be "realistic," but are tragically bent inward in their alienation from God.

As your eyes adjust to the spreading contagion, you see that fear torments them, filling their insides with anguish. Their folly has turned into fear as they feel alone and threatened. God feels absent to them, but he never leaves—they are willfully ignorant.

Some people seen in the vista below are part of the community of loyal lovers of God. They are companions who exude peace in God's presence and with one another. God feels present to them because they listen.

- *God the Father* is at work vetoing the plans of the disruptive agitators and power brokers.
- *Jesus* is extending comfort and shelter to those who will wake up to what is happening.
- The *Spirit* is whispering words of correction, relief, and renewal, guiding us to walk in love.

Some people are beginning to feel safe for the first time—their point of view has been interrupted by news they have never heard before. The news of unconditional love changes everything.

A word has come from the mountain of God. It is a spark of communal hope—God is rescuing the victims from their oppressors. He is also delivering the oppressors from their ignorance. He is letting them see him face-to-face.

Divine salvation has come for all. But not all are accepting this freedom. Nevertheless, it flows like a cleansing flood. Those who "know they are known" are glad and rejoicing. His kingdom has come, his will is being done by him, on earth as it is in heaven. This psalm is about changing you, not them. Grace sees your brokenness and turns you to hear the Living Word who delivers what he promises—himself.

Indwelling the Garden

[1]The fool has said in his heart, "There
is no God."
They are corrupt, they have committed detestable acts;
There is no one who does good.

Haughty pawns who are blind to God,
Let lies fly from their lips,
They smugly spout "God never was,"
While their lives reveal fraud's grip.

[2]The LORD has looked down from
heaven upon the sons of mankind
To see if there are any
who understand,
Who seek God.

Looking down with compassion's crown,
The Savior scans the land,
Searching for seekers with hearts attuned,
Who want to understand.

[3]They have all turned aside, together
they are corrupt;
There is no one who does good, not
even one.

Detours distract the surging crowd,
Their sanity unwinds,
They lost their way from the love's highway,
Faithfulness has gone blind.

[4] Do all the workers of injustice not
know,
Who devour my people as they eat
bread,
And do not call upon the LORD?

Palatial ignorance echoes full,
Their towers now grown cold,
They feed their bodies with insatiable deeds,
While they starve their crusty souls.

[5]There they are in great dread,
For God is with a righteous
generation.

Lightning splits the heavens,
Insecurity rains from the skies,
Shaking the boots of ruffians,
Beloved ones will rest as His prize.

[6] You would put to shame the plan of
the poor,
But the LORD is his refuge.

While hunters hound the poor
oppressed,
Seeking their weary prey,
In You is found a hiding place,
Where the cherished learn to
play.

[7] Oh, that the salvation of Israel *would come* out of Zion!
When the LORD restores the fortunes
of His people,
Jacob will rejoice, Israel will be
glad.

The circling dance of celebration,
Means your liberty's complete,
Good fortune's flow shall be restored,
Rejoice, you cheerful feet!

Taking Reflections with You

Let your heart leave this psalm hungry for wisdom and the life of blessing. The other option is to become critical and outraged—avoid that!

- What ideas came through *words* in this psalm that gave you a new perspective? What does it look and feel like to survey the world standing with Jesus?
- How did God's observation of the world help you to see him in a new way? How did God help you to understand the plight of humanity and the provision of *God's life* in a new way?
- How did this psalm reorient you? What did you discover about who you are, standing with Jesus in your observation, and *who you are* when you are not standing with Jesus? What are you committed to in your evaluation of others?
- What did the view from the balcony open up in your *relationship with God*? Could you see yourself going with him more often to survey the people in your life and keep you company?
- What can you hear Jesus say *now* that would have been judgment *before* this psalm, but now you can hear his words address you as hope of what can be?

- What do you need to release back to him as words to cleanse your soul from what has grown in you when you became a judge of others' faults?

Final Embrace

The discerning florist selects flowers that complement each other and create a vibrant cornucopia of color. Can you create an arrangement with dandelions, buttercups, and Scotch broom? Take weeds and make something wonderful. What colors can you bring to your world as you leave this psalm?

Wisdom lost.
What a cost.
Without.
Fools spout.
Love wrung out.
Existential emptiness.
No God.
Means me and my bod.
Lost consideration.
Me, my own creation.
Actually, I'm decaying.
Lost in straying.
Withered, fraying.
Colors are graying.
Everything decomposing.
But He sees.
Every detail.
Oversees.
Searching.
Scouting.
Finding someone doubting.
Looking.
Awakening.
Lives in the making.
My people.
Feeling love's pull.
Humming in the middle.
Getting their attention.
Never hesitation.
Overcoming fear's sensation.
Replaced with jubilation.
The safest place.
Know my face.
Zion's grace.
Future at the door.
What do You want more?
Restore?
Explore?
Turn.
Greet.
Me meeting You.

Psalm 15

Abiding with God's Presence

Lord, who may dwell in your sacred tent?
Who may live on your holy mountain?
(Psalm 15:1 NIV)

Surveying the Garden

Consider the difference between earning an embrace and being unconditionally embraced (pause now and read again).

Many forms of a "religious life" focus on human qualifications to enter God's blessings. Often, rituals replace the relational life—that way of being that resonates with the love of God.

We must scrub away any need to "condition God" so he will take us to himself. The gift of God's grace accepts us. We reside in God's garden by his gracious permission and nothing else.

We desire to live in communion with God and as companions with fellow humans, but our minds are conditional—we are not sure we are good enough.

One could see this psalm as a checklist for "measuring up" or a call to quit measuring oneself, despite our imperfections.

We may now leave behind any *conditions* for being loved. Then, we can explore the *consequences* of being and giving love. This dynamic transforms us for wholeness, faithfulness, and truthfulness. It creates a life-altering space when growth in sharing and bringing beauty is our quest.

This walk down the path takes us out of our self-imposed prison, where we strive for an appearance of perfection. We're embarking on a liberating pilgrimage of wonder and attentiveness.

We cannot earn intimacy with God. There is no value in investing in self-improvement, constraining our activities, or enduring and hoping for later payoffs. It does not work that way.

Obedience is beautiful when it flows from the joy of being loved by God. We reflect his beauty as the fruit of the Spirit, yielding in response to God's loving action.

God's way of being permeates and reverberates through those who confidently enter this meeting place with God. God's availability realigns us to join him with abandon, compelled by a love that does not look back, called by the joy of knowing the One who beckons to us.

Walk in wisdom, knowing it is not the words in your head or mouth, but in the Living Word who speaks, "Enter, friend," opening the doorway wide and inviting you to talk like friends, face-to-face. He says, "I want you to be with Me—always."

Into the Garden with God

This psalm can seem like a checklist to prepare ourselves to meet with God.

If we think meeting with God requires preapproval, as though we were buying a house, we will read the psalm as a guarded gate, intent on keeping the unworthy out and letting the top performers in.

Right from the start, we must acknowledge that Jesus is the only one who could live up to the standards outlined here.

Jesus has entered into our human sphere. He not only made a short visit, but he created a lasting, intertwined life of wholeness with God and humanity. This interwovenness continues.

This is not a psalm of judgment. It reflects on what it means to be a guest of God. As we are with him, we become transparent. God's goodness shines through our human thoughts, acts, and speech. When his light hits our rainy lives, rainbows appear.

The psalm focuses on the Tabernacle of God, the tent of meeting—the space where God and humans gather.

Jesus is now that meeting place. In John 1:14, the evangelist points to Jesus and says:

> And the Word became flesh, and dwelt among us; and we saw
> His glory, glory as of the only *Son* from the Father,
> full of grace and truth.
> (NASB)

Jesus is the One in whom we meet the living God. When we come to abide or dwell in him and he in us, he shines through us: he develops the fruit by his Spirit. Welcome to the meeting-place-in-God.

This psalm portrays who a person is "in Christ," living in him as our tent of meeting. This location is a dynamic place of cultivation facilitated by the Spirit—fruit follows.

Jesus invites you to spend time with him in his tent. The world is his tent. Also, he is a tent for you to indwell.

See Jesus now, as he sits in his tent and invites you to spend some transformative time as companions (which means to share bread: *com-* with/together, *pan-* bread).

Like a master baker, Jesus beckons you and says, "Come sit here for a while. Let's see what is possible for your life. Eat my bread and grow into sharing life with Me and your fellow humanity. Enter in, envision yourself fully alive, amazingly loved, and see how that reshapes your relationships.

Visions of Paradise

This is a tent of refreshing, a place to realize all that is possible when love has its way of motivating in life's interactions.

Along the Garden Path

As you approach God, you may feel incapable of connection. Many people read this psalm in that mode. We can embrace this encounter as receiving a gift. When God comes to you, hiding is impossible and a waste of letting wonder wash over you.

This psalm is for pilgrims and discoverers, a glimpse into personal reality.

God is personally present. God made access to himself in Jesus; consequently, we can see what has been made possible. Once you actually meet someone, a relationship becomes feasible rather than a fantasy.

The Holy Spirit brings us to be open to the light of God's glory. God's light penetrates into us, through us, and extends to others as we spend time in his shining place—his sanctuary.

In his presence, we develop a desire to love our neighbors. Our humanity transforms to act in the service of God, a Spirit-nurtured response to the love of God.

In God's kingdom, we become vessels of God's glory. We see the world beloved by God and are inspired to respond with our resonating activities of care.

Opportunities for nurturing healthy relationships open before our eyes. Hurtful interactions call us to restorative justice. Love ignites us to find courage—feeling our fear and doing the loving thing anyway.

This path embodies integrity. This commitment means consistency in what we think, feel, and do, which comes from an urge to love as Jesus loves.

A concern for our neighbors grows in our hearts, faithful to God's heart. We are becoming conformed to reality—meaning to God's love.

Conforming to God's love, we become available for secure friendships. The presence of God will purify us. His light will shine through the stained glass windows we are becoming. Others will sense God's presence in what becomes a holy place as we walk this sanctuaried path together.

You have been brought to God's gift of a holy place—filled with his presence to wake you up. Do not worry about yourself. The path ahead restores you to Jesus's presence—he will do the work. Fix your eyes on him; the rest will come into focus as you enter his tent.

Indwelling the Garden

1 LORD, who may reside in Your tent?
Who may settle on Your holy hill?

I'm searching again for Your intimate space,
Yearning for warmth in Your room.
A glimpse of glory shines through Your door;
All is prepared, but for whom?

2 One who walks with integrity, practices righteousness,
And speaks truth in his heart.

You welcome one with character sound,
Who gives beyond what's due.
Gazing fondly on integrity's child
Who speaks only words that are true.

3 He does not slander with his tongue,
Nor do evil to his neighbor,
Nor bring shame on his friend;

A cherished guest speaks words that bless,
Enhancing all who hear,
Undergirding fellow-lives,
And removing threatening fears.

4 A despicable person is despised in his eyes,
But he honors those who fear the LORD;
He takes an oath to his own detriment, and does not change;

Idolatrous lies He will revise;
Reverence is a compass true.
Ever faithful, always kind,
Steady with lavish virtue.

5 He does not lend his money at interest,
Nor does he take a bribe against the innocent.
One who does these things will never be shaken.

No advantage will he take,
Considerately helping a friend.
Joyous neighbors, he steadily makes;
He is faithful, right to the end.

Taking Reflections with You

Shed all the guilt you may feel for your inadequacy. Calm your focus and know that you are in the presence of the Spirit, who wants to cultivate good fruit in you.

- This psalm uses general and abstract words regarding what it means to be a good person. Where do you think goodness comes from? What words direct you?
- How did sitting with Jesus in his tent make you feel *about him*? What are you discovering about what God wants *for* you, not *from* you?
- Did this psalm impact how *you think about yourself* and what it means to find renewal in the "set-aside place of God"? Did you feel included or excluded? What does that say about *who you are*?
- As you consider leaving the tent of meeting, what is the state of your *relationship with God*? Do you feel acceptance and grace? Do you leave feeling empowered to more closely align with, resonate with, and be daily conformed to the life of Jesus?
- Did you *hear Jesus's invitation* to spend quality time with him and *hear his affirming* words?
- What would be *your request* of Jesus? Let him know what you need to feel able to enter his place of intimacy.

Final Embrace

Let the words below be a stepping stone, hopping toward the open tent, slow and savored in anticipation as the words emerge from your lips. Feel the hesitation if it is there in your soul. Why wouldn't you feel welcome? You belong in this place; read like you are finding home for the first time.

Walk in?
Your dwelling place?
And see Your face?

Your holy hill.
Resting still.
Withness.

Reverence.
Response.
Responsibility.
Reflecting joy.
Deflecting what destroys.
Integrity.
All of me.
Passionate solidarity.
Engaging reality.
Setting neighbors free.
Justly.
For everybody.
Kin.
Neighbors.
All humanity.
Resisting calamity.
Honoring civility.
Companions of God and me.

Affirming dignity.
I hear You say,
"I'll stand by you.
No matter what you do.
I'll be faithful and true.
When you're in need.
I'll fight all greed.
Hope I'll breed.
'Til you succeed.
Refined.
Aligned.
Purified with presence.
Exuding confidence.
Victorious.
Glorious.
Solid.
Secure."

Psalm 16

Resting in God's Path and Presence

You make known to me the path of life;
you will fill me with joy in your presence,
with eternal pleasures at your right hand.
(Psalm 16:11 NIV)

Surveying the Garden

Most of us are trying to get somewhere in life.

We survey an unknown horizon in the distance, except for the inevitability of death, which we all know is coming.

But right in front of us is the path we are on. This path winds through life and its many trials. We can see challenges exist on either side.

Glancing back, we find external struggles and internal memories of conflict. We wrestle with feeling valued, questioning whether we are taking the right paths.

This psalm wants to clarify your journey and give you confidence. Where you are going is not as important as who you go with. You need those who will grant dignity, hope, and a sense of sanity as traveling companions.

Life is not intended to be lived through inspirational sayings on your refrigerator. You need a companion who will sustain you—even past death. Meandering becomes meaningful with the right persons.

Withness matters. This psalm clarifies the difference between life without God and life with God.

God never leaves. Humans pursue other paths. They leave the source of life and suffer the consequences of being lost and alone. They roam adrift even though they are within the garden. They have no personal compass to guide them or discern their location.

We are invited now to follow the Path to Life. The path leads into the woods, but we have a guide. All those other options are still beckoning. But the Restoring One has gone before us and made the way to life. He is our safe passage.

Shed the world's hostility and accept the hospitable presence down the path; hear Jesus as he looks at you and says, "Here is the cup of connection; let's drink to our friendship."

Into the Garden with God

Psalm 16 is mentioned twice in the book of Acts. It points our attention to Jesus, expressing confidence that God's love will forever bring humans to a new humanity in Jesus. It was radical news then. It is often forgotten now.

On the day of Pentecost, Peter's sermon in Acts 2 reflects on this psalm. Peter can see David's deep confidence—specifically that death was not abandonment by God. Resurrection was promised.

This insight opens the way for finding final gladness, not the defeat of death. Peter derives the hope from this ancient witness and says:

> "But God raised him from the dead, putting an end to the agony of death, since it was impossible for Him to be held in its power.
> [25] For David says of him,
>
> *'I SAW THE LORD CONTINUALLY BEFORE ME,*
>
> *BECAUSE HE IS AT MY RIGHT HAND, SO THAT I WILL NOT BE SHAKEN.*
>
> *[26] THEREFORE MY HEART WAS GLAD AND MY TONGUE WAS OVERJOYED;*
>
> *MOREOVER MY FLESH ALSO WILL LIVE IN HOPE;*
>
> *[27] FOR YOU WILL NOT ABANDON MY SOUL TO HADES,*
>
> *NOR WILL YOU ALLOW YOUR HOLY ONE TO UNDERGO DECAY.*
>
> *[28] YOU HAVE MADE KNOWN TO ME THE WAYS OF LIFE;*

YOU WILL MAKE ME FULL OF GLADNESS WITH YOUR PRESENCE.'

29 "Brothers, I may confidently say to you regarding the patriarch David that he both died and was buried, and his tomb is with us to this day.
30 So because he was a prophet and knew that God had sworn to him with an oath to seat *one* of his descendants on his throne,
31 he looked ahead and spoke of the resurrection of the Christ, that He was neither abandoned to Hades, nor did His flesh suffer decay.
32 *It is* this Jesus *whom* God raised up, *a fact* to which we are all witnesses."

(Acts 2:24–32 NASB)

With Peter, we can find confidence. This assurance is grounded in an openness to the promise of a Guide who goes with us, before us, and who shelters and preserves us to the end and beyond.

Jesus does not need a compass and map to find the way; he is the way. Being with him and in his life is the destination. He is calling your name now to join him on the Path of Life.

Visions of Paradise

This path leads to a Life-giving destination. It is exquisite in its complexity and mystery, but it is not a challenge course; it is an abundant adventure with the One who loves to share journeys.

Along the Garden Path

In a world of insecurity, we are beckoned to stroll with the One who preserves our relational life in his sanctuaried presence. Walls and defense mechanisms fail to provide adequate security. Knowing we are with someone we can rely on is what matters.

We have come to be with our Maker, Mediator, and the Master of abundant life. Our welfare rests in his hands. Apart from him, we are less connected to life itself.

When separated, our emotions converge on self-preservation. You are intended to discover your delight and desires found and met in being *with* Jesus.

Other paths along the way seem to be inviting. Some people choose paths seeking beauty, wealth, and pleasure. Others focus on their family. Fulfillment can remain elusive. Some take detours into amusement, music, food, exotic adventures, or solitude. But these replacements for the real connection miss what actually sustains us in our faithful relationships.

In this sustaining relationship, your allegiance is a source of strength and joy, like a refreshing drink of life from the loving God.

The sacrament of friendship may include cups of coffee—these are important. The cup of Jesus's covenant holds the real wealth of being deeply connected.

Release any fear of needing to find the way by yourself. Open your ears to the wise counsel of the Spirit. You are being sculpted, starting with your heart, transforming as a whole person.

Jesus is close by at all times. His is a wraparound presence that brings peace. His love will transform your intentions, empowering you to live an exuberant life.

Are you afraid of death? You need to know that this Living God will never give up on you. Jesus has faced death and stands on the other side. He has experienced cruelty and corruption. He conquered the realm of death and will never leave you. He is the Path of Life who calls you to himself.

This psalm leaves us soaking in the Divine Presence. He has shown us his provision, protection, and promise of a resurrected life with him.

Now, gazing on his face, find the perpetual pleasure of personal existence as he intends. Trust in the Divine Guide who leads you to the Tree of Life on the Path of Life.

Shake the agitation and waves of frustration from your shoulders. Find rest, renewal, and restored delight. Jesus offers you his cup filled with the wine of grace. He offers it and says, "Take, drink, this is for you." Sip, breathe, and sing Eden's song from that first morning when the world began and all was fresh and new.

Indwelling the Garden

Unbrace yourself.

1 Protect me, God, for I take
refuge in You.

Shore up my soul against the tide,
Calm resting place, in You I hide.
In Your embrace all peace abides.
Ever living by Your side.

2 I said to the LORD, "You are my
LORD;
I have nothing good besides You."

You alone, my final home,
Bone of my bone, LORD of Shalom,
There's nowhere else I'd rather roam.
Secure under Your giving dome.

3 As for the saints who are on the
earth,
They are the majestic ones; all my
delight is in them.

Allied friends shall faithfully sing,
Together joined, our praises bring.
Delight shall soar like an eagle's wing.
Free as an awakened spring.

4 The pains of those who have
acquired another god will be
multiplied;
I will not pour out their drink
offerings of blood,
Nor will I take their names upon my
lips.

The wingless mourn of earthbound
states,
Ensnared by fowler's alluring bait,
Now enslaves them with sorrow's
weight,
Lost in a tragic fate.

5 The LORD is the portion of my inheritance and my cup;
You support my lot.

My goblet brims with joy in You,
Future bliss now springs to view,
Included forever in Your life, so true,
Your hope is my horizon's view.

6 The measuring lines have fallen for me in pleasant places;
Indeed, my inheritance is beautiful to me.

A well-trimmed hedge now frames my land,
All that I have comes from Your hand.
At the end of my journey with You, I'll stand,
Joined with an angel band.

7 I will bless the LORD who has advised me;
Indeed, my mind instructs me in the night.

Your name shall shape my lips like a kiss.
Your patient counsel guides me to bliss,
My mind directed so not to miss,
Saved from the night's abyss.

8 I have set the LORD continually before me;
Because He is at my right hand, I will not be shaken.

Aligned with Your presence, I walk Your way;
You keep me forever from going astray.
Confident and strong, I will obey,
Dawning with a bright new day.

9 Therefore my heart is glad and my glory rejoices;
My flesh also will dwell securely.

Celebration adorns my soul,
Flags of hope fly, red carpets unroll;
My body tingles as You make all things whole,
Glad in Your heart's true pull.

10 For You will not abandon my soul to Sheol;
You will not allow Your Holy One to undergo decay.

Your rejection, I will never fear,
Nor decay in the grave, drawing ever near,
My assurance is strong; in You, I'm secure,
Your grace will never disappear.

[11] You will make known to me the way
of life;
In Your presence is fullness of joy;
In Your right hand there are
pleasures forever.

You disclose life's mysteries day
by day,
Exploring new pathways now and
always,
I delight in Your joy as it comes to
play,
Knowing You are with me to stay.

Taking Reflections with You

Hopefully, joy bubbles forth from your soul. Watch them float and catch colors as they evoke the rainbow's promise of perpetual renewal.

- What images in this psalm stand out to you? What hopeful vision do you have?
- How was the deepest desire of God made available for you? Did you find insights that helped you to see God in a new way?
- What would it look like to see Jesus as your path and discover *who you are* as a person who belongs on this path?
- Do you know where your current path is taking you in *your relationship with* God? Is it enriching your relationships with God and those who are important to you?
- What restful words can you hear the Father *say to you*?
- What grateful words does the Spirit bring to you *as a response*?

Final Embrace

The pathways of our lives often feel blocked by locked doorways. We feel the resistance of an unfriendly face, a tone of voice that batters, or a silence that feels immensely thick. The paths of acceptance are welcoming and life-transforming. Stride forward with slow, long steps to feel the movement within.

Lifeways.
Ignored ways.
Lost on freeways.
Wondering how love plays.
Looking for security.
Thinking You can set me free.
With only You beside me.
I know what You said to me.
Loving your friends.
Life easily upends.
On You I can depend.
You are delight.
Even in the night.
Quenching the fright.
While others drink their plight.
Allegiance to whom?
You or the world gone zoo?
I share the cup with You.
You're my space.
Face to face.
Unbounded loving place.
Heart overflowing grace.
Following Your trail.
Even when I fail.
You're love's perfect portrayal.
In travail.
You prevail.
Death may assail.
But decay You curtail.
All alive.
Heart.
Pulse.
Lips.
Every inch.
Tingling alive.
Avoiding the pit.
Missing the abyss.
Gifted.
Confusion untwisted.
Clarity.
Ahead of me.
It's You.
Before me.
Behind me.
Beside me.
Around me.
Inside me.
Soul-surround.
Free.

Psalm 17

Care for a Bruised Apple

Keep me as the apple of your eye;
hide me in the shadow of your wings.
(Psalm 17:8 NIV)

Surveying the Garden

Along life's journey, it would be nice to be cherished. Too often, we feel bruised or taken for granted.

As innocent children, we enter the world without many expectations. We delight whenever cared for in an enduring way. That is called being the "apple of someone's eye," being seen and focused on with pleasure.

As time passes, others expect us to meet their standards of behavior or fulfill their needs. The innocence of being an adorable child fades. We hear much of what is missing or needs work. We become weary in the garden of our life.

We wish to be seen as whole and innocent again, unconditionally loved for who we are. We desire to be a beloved and valued child. We stride forward, knowing belovedness is always a possibility.

My wife notices homeless people, thinking, "He is some mother's beloved child." This perspective reveals that they were the apple of someone's eye at some point.

This psalm invites us to look again and see the fallen apples, the cherished apples, and the apples that do not fall far from the tree.

Jesus sees you and says, "You are the delight of my eye and the treasure of My heart. You need to hear those words over and over again. I want you to have those words emblazoned on your mind so your heart can hear them when you see My face. I am so very fond of you. Come sit under that apple tree with me for a while."

Into the Garden with God

This psalm reflects the tension between being embraced and being effaced by our oppressors.

Jesus has promised to be with us always. He sent his Spirit to awaken us to love and know we are children of his Abba.

We encounter the face of God reflected in Jesus, who affirms us. However, based on worldly values, standards, and expectations, we let the world judge our inadequacy. This is bruising.

Dark mirrors distort reality—regarding both God and ourselves. Those mirrors lie. We need to see ourselves reflected in Jesus's face. By his Spirit, we hear, "You are Mine, the apple of My eye."

The book of Revelation alludes to Psalm 17 with this face-to-face image, promising bright and bold:

> They will see His face, and His name *will be* on their foreheads.
> (Revelation 22:4 NASB)

Our faces are transformed when meeting another person who adores us. It is the gaze of delight when reuniting with a long-absent friend. You are unconditionally adored.

Revelation's visions are full of bruised people who find joy at the journey's end. This psalm is a foretaste of that being seen and cherished. Prepare to be seen as a shining apple falling into the hands of the One who made you, even with your bruises from along the journey.

Jesus has a place for you under that apple tree. To him, every piece of fruit is loved, and so are you.

Visions of Paradise

Along the Garden Path

The path of this psalm takes you as you are, with all your fears, failures, and defensiveness.

Your body, eyes, lips, mouth, feet, and everything that moves are personally involved.

The Living God pays attention. You would love to bend God's ear; he is eagerly focused. You especially want your honesty to be met by his caring attentiveness.

This passionate psalm is not desperate but is confident. The outcome depends on knowing the love and capacity of the One who loves freely. His words engage the heart. Do you feel yours is held?

We often believe we are as innocent or as guiltless as a human can be. We see what others miss.

We want our activities to be met with a voice of approval—at least concluding that we had the right heart. And that is where we are going as this psalm delves into our deep places—even with blindness to our dark side.

This psalm reflects being with One who *revives, not judges*. We may experience a "dark night of the soul" in the loneliness of tough times, but not without being refined. In the morning sun, we are prepared for new forms of health. Our inmost decay gives way to external fruitfulness.

In most of life, what others do is not under your control. Babblers and brutes may wear you away into confusion. You can walk the other way. Torah provides another way, not as a set of rules but a shared path with God and others. The heart and feet start working together.

This walk is not a pilgrimage without pain but a path of participation with a gracious companion. All you want to say will be heard. You will make it to the end. You want assurance that you will reach the beauty yet to come. It is already found in him.

The greatest show on earth is expressed in his acts of loving-kindness. God is faithful to his promises. He extends his love and uses the power of his might. He will rescue. He will provide a refuge. He will guard you in the wilderness.

We are sheltered in the embrace of encircling wings, not unlike the wings of the cherubim above the mercy seat, perched above the Ark of the covenant. We are safe in the shade of personal, persistent liberation and mercy.

The present crisis is past. Comfort has come. The battles are ended. The God who heals generations of brokenness invites you to shed the bandages and bruises. Discover health anew in meeting him eye to eye.

As you gaze on him, you will be transformed into his likeness. This is a moment of waking up to reality, enjoying a satisfaction that brings joyful eyes. All is right with God, and the world will be right when it is attuned to his presence.

He is attentive and ready—enter.

Indwelling the Garden

1 Hear a just cause, LORD, give Your
attention to my cry;
Listen to my prayer, which is not
from deceitful lips.

Attend to my innocent, weeping wail,
As I spill my honorable grief.
Pour Your mercy on my passionate
plea,
Let my honesty bring Your relief.

2 Let my judgment come forth from
Your presence;
Let Your eyes look with integrity.

Your pardon's release provides pure
peace,
Your word brings dignity true.
Impartial to all, You attend to the
small;
Your deep-seeing gaze will renew.

3 You have put my heart to the test;
You have visited *me* by night;
You have sifted me and You find
nothing;
My intent is that my mouth will not
offend.

Delicate yield to refining revealed,
Nightly, I wait here so still.
You test 'til all's well, which moves me
to tell
What Your infinite beauty instills.

4 As for the works of mankind, by the
word of Your lips
I have kept from the ways of the
violent.

Devilish deeds are kept in check,
For Your word is my shield to
protect.
Treading no more on long-spoiled soil,
You guide me in trust and respect

5 My steps have held to Your paths.
My feet have not slipped.

I trust Your trail over summit and vale,
You set my pace to Your stride.
Your well-worn tracks cross a mountain
pass,
Never sliding down dangerous
hillsides.

6 I have called upon You, for You will answer me, God;
Incline Your ear to me, hear my speech.

My requests shall flow from humble lips,
Your ready response I'll await.
Lend me Your ear to my creeping fear,
Come before it is too late.

7 Show Your wonderful faithfulness,
Savior of those who take refuge at Your right hand
From those who rise up *against them*.

Grandiose is Your generous love,
Displayed with an awesome reveal.
Paradise enfolds within Your hold,
Exhilarates, calms, and heals.

8 Keep me as the apple of the eye;
Hide me in the shadow of Your wings

Standing adored as Your affection's reward,
As a cherished kernel of Joy,
You shelter me firm in the wings of dawn,
Your care and concern full employed.

9 From the wicked who deal violently with me,
My deadly enemies who surround me.

I feel such fear on brutal paths,
Danger on every side.
When oppression excels, encircling me,
In Your harbor, I will abide.

10 They have closed their unfeeling *hearts*,
With their mouths they speak proudly.

Cold hearts forget love's cherishing art,
Thinking of selfish gain,
Their tongues progress as plans for distress,
Extending their neighbor's pain.

11 They have now surrounded us in our steps;
They set their eyes to cast *us* down to the ground.

These battles rage like wildfire,
They're licking at my door.
Destruction follows their edicts,
To toss me to the floor.

12 He is like a lion that is eager to tear,
And as a young lion lurking in secret places.

Wild animals hunt all around,
Hungry for their prey,
Prowling cool in the shadows deep,
Keeping us at bay.

[13] Arise, LORD, confront him, make
him bow down;
Save my soul from the wicked with
Your sword,

Emerge, LORD Victor! Tame the beasts,
Cage the snarling brutes.
Subdue, with skill, the ferocious fiends.
Tamed as Your love refutes.

[14] From people by Your hand, LORD,
From people of the world, whose
portion is in *this* life,
And whose belly You fill with Your
treasure;
They are satisfied with children,
And leave their abundance to their
babies.

Emancipate my war-torn scars,
From those who waged for gain,
Gorged from all stored up for them,
Their bellies burst in pain.

[15] As for me, I shall behold Your face
in righteousness;
I shall be satisfied with Your likeness
when I awake.

Feast my eyes on the early sunrise,
'Til my sight is filled with You.
Brightened by Your song to greet the
dawn,
Refreshed by Your presence's dew.

Taking Reflections with You

Hopefully, you are finding healing with a new heading. Try glimpsing the different you, waking up to what is becoming possible.

- Did any words or phrases awaken your ears and mind? Could you feel this psalm in your body?
- How did this psalm help you to see God in a new way? Do you feel that he is *for* you and *with* you?
- How did this psalm help you see *who you are*? Can you see yourself as the apple of his eye? Who is the apple of your eye? Do they know?
- What does sitting under the apple tree say about your *relationship with God*? Do you sense you can freely talk to God, unconditionally accepted?

- What tender words did you hear from him, or would you like to hear from him?
- What appreciative words would you like to reflect back?

Final Embrace

Fruit grows when the conditions are right. For you, walking in the sun, being nourished by the rain, trimming away what is in the way, and other forms of receiving and giving yourself care are essential. Speak these words with honesty and hope.

Innocent.
I am spent.
Hearken.
Listen.
Justly attend.
Pity me.
Hear my plea.
Distressfully.
Let Your eyes see.
Exonerate me.
Set me free.
I'm not guilty.
My heart split.
I'm open wide.
Visit inside.
Nothing to hide.
I've tried and tried.
May this silent night,
Find me right.
Refine to bright.
To be Your delight.
Kept from harm.
Neighborhood alarms.
Choices to crazy farms.
Rejecting so that hate disarms.
Big steps.
Your path.
A loving math.
With pleasure's aftermath.
Guided by Your craft.
Compass set.
Not there yet.
Mercy is most evident.
Where grace is finally met.
Sunrise and sunset.
Glory reset.
Cherishing moment.
Eye-to-eye endearment.
Embracing fulfillment.
Concealed in contentment.
Close up.
Filled up.
Set up.
Rise up.
Delivered up.
Faced up.
To You.
Bliss renew.
Awakened.

Psalm 18

Finding the Depths of Divine Intimacy and Otherness

He brought me out into a spacious place;
he rescued me because he delighted in me.
(Psalm 18:19 NIV)

Surveying the Garden

They are the sweetest words: "I love you."

Yet, they are but a shadow of the encountered reality we hope for, engaging the heart of another.

We want real life with another, touching all the scars, stories, safety, and sacrifices. We want the satisfaction of being fully embraced. The words recall but cannot fully renew the ecstasy of those moments of fulfillment.

Versions of those elements are etched deep in our memories. Intuitively, they create a yearning for a unique connection for every relationship. Much of life involves longing for love appropriate to each relationship, or we grow weary in the waiting.

Psalm 18 is a whirlwind of crisis intervention, connection, and emotionally glimpsing the heights of wonder and plumbing the depths of shaken foundations. It is not a peaceful psalm.

In this psalm, God makes sense of intimacy as an awareness of his companionship. It also reveals God's absolute otherness as the Master of the Universe. Otherness is not distance; it is differentiation meeting us where we are. Differentiation means acknowledging differences that maintain or deepen the connection.

God is the One who shapes and shakes the earth and nations. He is the safe center of the universe. In the end, he delivers all his creation from what ails it—he is the God who brings fulfillment—with a love that will not let us go.

God makes a secure place for us. God is not just a big rock to sit on. He is the haven where no threat can intrude. This psalm-space is the work of God, created in places of natural beauty and danger.

This sanctuary is a hideaway where we are restored from what disturbs our world.

Jesus himself is this place of retreat. We are called to abide in him. Sitting with him, we wonder at all he made and all that clashes within it. He is the calm in the chaos.

This place in the garden is high and wondrous. From it, we see how vast the garden is. Breathe in and notice there is no fear here. We primarily sense the intimate presence of One who has been through it all. He has brought you to this place to be with him.

Prepare to go on a roller coaster of sensations as you face storms, obstacle courses, heights, meadows, and the entrance of God to create some majestic moments. Jesus offers you his hand and suggests, "You might want to buckle the seat belt of your soul; we are going on an adventure." And so you hear the click, close your eyes, and feel the thrill of being lifted upward.

Into the Garden with God

You may identify with this psalm by focusing on the author's desired deliverance.

This psalm also turns our attention to God's intervention on behalf of the world. We stand with Jesus in a high mountain vista, safe and secure. We will share in wonder, looking through the eyes of the One we stand with.

Paul borrowed from this psalm when writing his majestic letter to the Romans. Interestingly, he did not extract its anxiety. Paul finds a reason to celebrate God's friendship and his intention for intervention regarding the welfare of humanity.

Paul sees a light from the mountain that brings inspiration. This psalm's ancient proclamation announces good news to the nations. The love and mercy of God are comprehensive in their message. So Paul, a Hebrew, finds confidence in God's revelation to be for all peoples, consistent over the ages, and he states,

And for the Gentiles to glorify God for his mercy; as it is written:
"THEREFORE I WILL GIVE PRAISE TO YOU AMONG THE
GENTILES, AND I WILL SING PRAISES TO YOUR NAME."
(Romans 15:9 NASB)

Paul is amazed at how all people are addressed by grace.

We stand here with Paul, seeing the otherworldliness of God. With Paul, we notice hope for the nations.

We also stand here with Jesus, ready to discover hope for the world so they will know they are loved in a transformative way by the Otherly God who accompanies all peoples.

Jesus's voice echoes like a waterfall across the cliffs, crags, and clefts in the rock. He says, "I am alive! I have faithful love for you! I will bring you to a wide and open place where we can be free for and with each other. Come higher up and further into Me!" Imagine yourself feeling free, leaping like a deer or a mountain goat, finding joy in the wonder of the wild with One who loves to share it all.

Visions of Paradise

Jesus safely harbors us in this place of refuge and restoration beside rushing waterfalls and far above the terrain spread out below. This place within his care is for rest and preparation to run some obstacle courses—but not alone. He says, "Come with Me, and I will show you how close I can be." Proceed with wonder.

Along the Garden Path

This is a long path. Psalm 18 is the fourth longest of all the Psalms, with fifty verses! It contains moments of rest and comfort, but also stretches running, panting, and fighting off challengers.

Like a runner in the starting blocks, one looks down the path. With focused passion, one presses on with delight to reach the One at the other end.

The setting is wrapped in wildness. Torrents of water and stormy skies texture the backdrop of turbulence.

But along the journey, the curtains of heaven open. The Master of storms comes down to meet you right where you are. Jesus breaks through the clouds, and the brightness of his presence expels every fleeing patch of darkness.

And then his voice sounds forth. All creation seems to be torrential waters; lightning and pouring rain all seem to rise to meet his entrance.

He reaches down to lift you out of the calamity of the moment. In that touch, you feel the thinness between heaven and earth. Love has opened the way that matters most.

Where are you lifted to? A wide-open space, a meadow made for running, to be set free in the roominess of beauty. This glade is a fully alive space where streams run and seasons constantly change their garb.

You feel so clean. You love that your hearts beat together. He draws you alongside to share his strides. You love to hear the deep tones of his comforting voice. Such qualities can only spring from a majestically humble heart.

His words guide you. You listen. You feel complete as you move at Godspeed—slowly savoring every step together.

You cannot imagine wanting to be anywhere else. Who but this God could make this path so wild and safe simultaneously?

You arrive at a high and hidden cleft in the rock. The noise of waterfalls serenades the setting. The world is spread out like a picnic tablecloth, inviting the nations to come and share a meal, make a memory, and become members of this family of the beloved.

You want to shout out, but you think they cannot hear. He tells you to shout it out anyway—it is an ancient and ever-new announcement that may be carried on the wind to waiting ears.

You feel free. Then it hits you. The Living God is alive. He is right here with you. His unshakable love conquers all and makes all things work for good.

And then you start to sing. You feel that you could sing of this selfless love forever. You feel chosen to stand with King David, who had a heart after God. He had a long and wearying trail to ascend—but he did not give up running or singing.

You feel the music rising in you like the morning sun. It spills over the horizon as you release what is welling up inside.

Indwelling the Garden

1 "I love You, Lord, my strength."

All my kindling affections
Ignite in Your infinite close.
Flame of Indwelling One-to-one
You sustain the stretching cosmos.

2 The Lord is my rock and my fortress and my savior,
My God, my rock, in whom I take refuge;
My shield and the horn of my salvation, my stronghold.

Hide me in Your hallowed halls,
Safe within Your hold;
Fortify me from the fray,
Encompass and enfold.

3 I call upon the Lord, who is worthy to be praised,
And I am saved from my enemies.

I entreat You, Dear Defender,
Who instills within me thanks,
Please shelter me from thickets
Of my enemy's threatening ranks.

4 The ropes of death encompassed me,
And the torrents of destruction terrified me.

I'm caught in the snare of death's cruel sneer,
Now bristling me with fear,
Flooded with terror that tears me apart,
With haters crushing near.

5 The ropes of Sheol surrounded
me;
The snares of death confronted
me.

6 In my distress I called upon
the LORD,
And cried to my God for help;
He heard my voice from His temple,
And my cry for help before Him
came into His ears.

7 Then the earth shook and quaked;
And the foundations of the mountains were trembling
And were shaken, because He was
angry.

8 Smoke went up out of His nostrils,
And fire from His mouth was
devouring;
Coals burned from it.

9 He also bowed the heavens down
low, and came down
With thick darkness under His feet.

10 He rode on a cherub and flew;
And He sped on the wings of the
wind.

11 He made darkness His hiding
place, His canopy around Him,
Darkness of waters, thick clouds.

The hiss of Death leans to my ear
Freezing my heartbeat cold.
Despair darkens my rolling tears,
While my quaking breath I hold.

Collapsing exhausted, I gasp for You,
A waning murmur for help.
This choke is all I can muster;
My fading, final yelp.

The world is a turbulent tossing
Of earthquakes that You send.
Volcanoes erupt, the mountains shudder,
While Your truth You still defend.

An ashen explosion has dimmed my
view,
Lava came pouring down,
As Your justice consumes all rebellion,
Like a wildfire, defiance was
drowned.

Splitting the sky, You entered,
Stepping on this restless land.
Your presence covered the mountains,
Which storms could not withstand.

You're gathered here with angel hosts,
An adoring, attendant envoy.
Buoyant together on the dancing
breeze
With Your inaugural wind of Joy.

Pavilioned in a mystery steep,
Thick majesty surrounds,
Filling up the ocean deep,
While rolling thunder pounds.

12 From the brightness before Him
passed His thick clouds,
Hailstones and coals of fire.

Flashing light then shears the night,
The clouds unfurl their load.
Frozen rain now salts the ground,
And the blizzard hides the road.

13 The LORD also thundered in the
heavens,
And the Most High uttered His voice,
Hailstones and coals of fire.

Your thunderclap still rumbles on,
Echoing across the plain.
Your whisper roars, resounding still,
Your royalty explained.

14 He sent out His arrows, and
scattered them,
And lightning flashes in abundance,
and routed them.

The bow is bent, the point is set,
Now streaking across the ground.
From flashing fingers, light fans out,
Followed by dislodging sounds.

15 Then the channels of water
appeared,
And the foundations of the world
were exposed
By Your rebuke, LORD,
At the blast of the breath of Your
nostrils.

You bathe the earth with glittering
floods,
And the geysers shoot up high.
Conductor of earth's symphony
Your splendor fills the sky.

16 He sent from on high, He took me;
He drew me out of many waters.

When rumpled, beaten by the flood,
Your hands came to my side,
Lifting my limp and listless frame,
I'm plucked from the crushing tide.

17 He saved me from my strong
enemy,
And from those who hated me, for
they were too mighty for me.

Sure my life was at an end,
Resigned, I closed my eyes;
Instead, You extended your encircling
hold,
My contenders were made to fly.

18 They confronted me in the day of
my disaster,
But the LORD was my support.

Those bullied, bruised, broken days,
Are now a fading dream,
Now, the rush of reviving ways
Dance me to share Your schemes.

19 He also brought me out into
an open place;
He rescued me, because He delighted in me.

I'm rolling now in meadows green,
All painted with profusion's hues,
Frolicking with Your Jubilee joy,
Basking in Your gladness anew.

20 The LORD has rewarded me
according to my righteousness;
According to the cleanness of my
hands He has repaid me.

21 For I have kept the ways of
the LORD,
And have not acted wickedly
against my God.

22 For all His judgments were before
me,
And I did not put away His statutes
from me.

23 I was also blameless with Him,
And I kept myself from my
wrongdoing.

24 Therefore the LORD has repaid me
according to my righteousness,
According to the cleanness of my
hands in His eyes.

25 With the faithful You show
Yourself faithful;
With the blameless You prove
Yourself blameless;

26 With the pure You show
Yourself pure,
And with the crooked You show
Yourself astute.

Affirmation flows in these evening glows,
While reflecting on days well-lived.
You gladsome say You respect my ways;
Cherished, in Your love, I'm hid.

I have tried and stayed true, listening
to You,
Walking along by Your side.
Averting again that death call to sin,
Knowing I fill You with pride.

What's first on my mind is the path You
define,
My compass, I try to keep poised.
Resisting to choose—not to wander
or lose—
reckless roads or cunning decoys.

Integrity's flag forever I'll wave,
Living ever true to my word.
With feet firmly planted against foul
winds,
Life without You would feel absurd.
Affirmation flows in the evening glow,
Reflecting on well-lived days.
You delightfully say You observe my
way,
Cherishing me under Your gaze.

Mirror of mild, mild in the mirror,
I reflect Your patient embrace,
Wholly for the whole, who live by Your
scroll,
Transformed by the sight of Your
face.

Honor You display to the honorable,
For the meek, You gently decide,
Frustration You create for those who
frustrate,
Who always seem to deride.

27 For You save an afflicted people,
But You humiliate haughty eyes.

Your constant return to rescue the spurned,
Saves the trampled, tired, and torn.
But the arrogant fool You slowly do cool,
To freeze out conceit overgrown.

28 For You light my lamp;
The LORD my God illumines my darkness.

My candle burns in the dead of night,
It can only be lit by You,
My only hope, to curb the fright,
Was the bright Your presence threw.

29 For by You I can run at a troop of warriors;
And by my God I can leap over a wall.

Vitality comes in the early morn,
To face another mess.
I approach each pile of irksome toils,
With Your help, my strength is blessed.

30 As for God, His way is blameless;
The word of the LORD is refined;
He is a shield to all who take refuge in Him.
31 For who is God, but the LORD?
And who is a rock, except our God,

Truer than another dawn,
Your promise bonds my day.
Your shelter gives me room to roam,
To work and take time to play.
You alone can claim the throne,
Master of the Great Unknown.
Your steady bedrock undergirds,
As our constant cornerstone.

32 The God who encircles me with strength,
And makes my way blameless?

I'm hewn by the Shaper of Human Souls,
Your breath sculpts ever-new.
You saw potential deep within,
By Your grace, my heart-strength grew.

33 He makes my feet like deer's *feet*,
And sets me up on my high places.

I'm a prancing goat on a mountain slope,
You make me frolic in Spring.
I give the thanks due, surveying the view,
A panorama that makes my heart sing.

34 He trains my hands for battle,
So that my arms can bend a bow of bronze.

You prepare me for the daily duel,
To live a balanced life,
Teaching skills to meet life's blows,
While loving both work and wife.

35 You have also given me the shield
of Your salvation,
And Your right hand upholds me;
And Your gentleness makes me
great.

You protect me from the petty plagues
Coming in ruinous raids.
You shield me safe within Your palm,
While dispelling the renegades.

36 You enlarge my steps under me,
And my feet have not slipped.

I'm running secure on the mountain
ridge,
Striding steadily on the rise.
My trust in You gives me cause to jump,
Leaping freely with joy improvised.

37 I pursued my enemies and
overtook them,
And I did not turn back until they
were consumed.

Victory is a gift from You,
You see the battle through,
Never to find myself in flight,
While You fix what's gone askew.

38 I shattered them, so that they
were not able to rise;
They fell under my feet.

39 For You have encircled me with
strength for battle;
You have forced those who rose up
against me to bow down under me.

I commit to tame the wild ones,
'Til fears are calmly caged.
I mute the mockers in their taunt
And silence rebellion's rage.
I'm prepared to nullify
The tyrants of distress,
Energized to win the prize,
And defeat those who oppress.

40 You have also made my enemies
turn their backs to me,
And I destroyed those who hated
me.

I triumphed in the day of strife
And quelled the clashing crowd.
Tranquil now, to You I bow,
Having hushed that clamorous
cloud.

41 They cried for help, but there was
no one to save,
They cried to the LORD, but he did
not answer them.

Assistance did not come for them,
Who cried when near defeat.
Their careers of chaos finally dimmed
When Your discipline was complete.

42 Then I beat them fine like the dust
before the wind;
I emptied them out like the mud of
the streets.

They turned to dust, blown by a gust,
With the turning sands of time.
Their forgotten tunes fill empty ruins,
With no honor for their crimes.

43 You have rescued me from the contentions of the people;
You have placed me as head of the nations;
A people whom I have not known serve me.

Your garment of Peace will now increase,
Contention has ceased in the land.
You lift me to drink Your victory cup,
And preside over roving bands.

44 As soon as they hear, they obey me;
Foreigners pretend to obey me.

Serenity sweet, I sit at Your feet,
While the nations feel your sway.
Some live from the heart, a few play a part,
In the end, all will obey.

45 Foreigners lose heart,
And come trembling out of their fortresses.

Their hearts fade away when defeat comes their way,
With nowhere left to fly,
Warriors will kneel, deep sorrow they'll feel,
Their tears will flow as they cry.

46 The LORD lives, and blessed be my rock;
And exalted be the God of my salvation,

You're my Lively Victor, my supporting stone,
I love to sing Your acclaim,
My tune shall circle around the moon
As Your healing life, I proclaim.

47 The God who executes vengeance for me,
And subdues peoples under me.

Ever present, You're my release,
You saved me from the fray.
Humbled hordes of my enemies,
Have ceased their destructive play.

48 He rescues me from my enemies;
You indeed lift me above those who rise up against me;
You rescue me from a violent man.

Now I live in quietude, my life renewed,
Above the strong-armed stress.
Gone, the invaders who spoiled my rest,
I'm released, delighted, and blessed.

49 Therefore I will give thanks to You among the nations, LORD,
And I will sing praises to Your name.

Appreciation breathes new inspiration,
As I shout Your wonders wide.
Lifting Your Name, I sing of Your fame,
Echoing through the countryside.

50 He gives great salvation to His king,
And shows faithfulness to His anointed,
To David and his descendants forever.

My constant companion in this Kingly court,
Your compassion pours out long.
Chosen for service, Your servant kneels,
Forever to sound your song.

Taking Reflections with You

What a workout of emotions! Hopefully, you stayed safe huddling in the cleft of the rock or leaping in the expansive open meadows.

- What *images* in this psalm gave you a sense of the nearness and distance of God, awakening new thoughts for you in your struggles?
- How did showing up to engage the challenges of the world surprise you? Did you see *who God is* in any new way amid the turmoil?
- Did this psalm bring any past or present trauma to your mind? Did you see *who you are or how you have been shaped* as the psalm touched your heart's tender places? Where is your safe place? Who is your safe person?
- What did this psalm make visible and visceral for you in your *relationship with God*? Do you find any intimacy (meaning deep closeness) in the wonder of the otherness of God (meaning One who cannot be contained in human words or thoughts)?
- What words of comfort and security did you hear offered to you by God?
- What deeply buried feelings could you release in words long concealed that need to be spoken and heard by the One who holds you?

Final Embrace

Intimacy is a definition of health in the world of personal relations. It is not limited to the physical; it is a heart condition. You know it is happening when joy comes from knowing that you are known and discovering that you are delighted in. Let this vision compel you forward.

Intervention.
Halfway to heaven.
Exodus reinvention.
Needing Your intercession.
Depths of despair.
Heights of repair.
Evernear.
Everfar.
Wherever I go, You are.
I love, adore.
Want so much more.
Haven of hope.
Up every slope.
Secure my rope.
Safe and sound.
On rocking ground.
Swirling around.
'Til I am found.
In You.
"Help!" I cry.
To catch Your eye.
To bend Your ear.
Needing You near.
Then.
Open sky.
Down You fly.
Your love applied.
Brilliant reply.
Your presence supply.
Your voice.
Says I'm Your choice.
My bursting heart, rejoice.
I'm Your delight.
In wide-open sight.
Dancing on the heights.
Flipped upright.
'Cause with You I'm right.
We're friends.
That never ends.
Clean in heart.
Clean in hands.
Clear 'til each other understands.
No hiding from each other.
Clearly clear.
Nearest near.
Safest safe.
My hiding place.
Trained to be.
Forever free.
As You and me.
Shedding fear.
Welfare dear.
Alive.
We thrive.
In this buzzing hive.
'Til we arrive.
Singing our liveliest jive.
Once again.
Revived.

Psalm 19

Light to See the World and God's Ways

The heavens declare the glory of God;
the skies proclaim the work of his hands.
(Psalm 19:1 NIV)

Surveying the Garden

We start today by looking up. Yes, we begin by looking at the sky. But then we will look through what is seen and listen to the One who makes it all. There is a voice from beyond.

We are learning to hear beyond the visible to the personal that holds it all together. That is what you do with every word you read on this page. Every word points to a deeper reality. Your name points to you.

We love the beauty of the world. We learn to appreciate its wonder.

Imagine a time-lapse video of the sun running for five to ten seconds. It starts with a brilliant sunrise, arching to high noon, and then sinking to a glorious sunset. That brief mindful art encounters the world as a day imaginatively captured.

Now see the moon rise, orange in the early night sky, then arcing over the top, flanked by stars, and finally setting in the west. It is a mysterious gift lighting the night and tugging at the tides. You are reflecting on reality.

Next, imagine the Torah (the account of God's beginnings in the Old Testament) as a light-emitting text, a scroll, or a book. See it also telling a big arching story, including your limited lifespan from birth to the end, hopefully with family gathered around.

That Torah story big picture is the enlightening context revealing God's provision and presence. It was written to invite you into the big story as "the way" (the meaning of Torah) to bring your life to the fullest joy.

Finally, see your inner life infused with light, initiated and sustained by the Creator. The light of his presence allows us to see the works of creation as his hospitable care. Your inner life is given light from him as a gift. Creation is another gift, including those you love. All is grace.

Your inner life is not separate from these layers of light—it is the faith awakened in us because of God's faithfulness and the faithful creation he maintains. Faith dawns as we discern the gift and the Giver. That is the invitation of Psalm 19.

As children, we grow in the context of the changing days and nights. Our parents teach us about the world. We are full of curiosity and wonder. Our memories, musings, and mutterings all converge as we grow.

When we discover the One who loved us from the start, it could be a moment of joy, awakening to what was always there. A light has guided us, but we could not always understand how it illuminated our way. This psalm cracks open what is hidden for light to break through.

Now you stand looking up, peering into the light of the glory of God, making this moment wondrous as you see that everything points to his work, ways, and the wonder of his presence.

Jesus beckons you; his hand seems to light the way and urge you to follow his prompt.

Into the Garden with God

This psalm surprises us by opening our eyes and ears to see and hear good news.

With gratitude, we enter this path lit from above, behind, and in front of us, lighting our life's path throughout the garden.

When Paul looks at the heavens, he recognizes that many people miss out on some excellent news as God displays his glory. He believes people must be spiritually blind, missing what God has done in making himself known. It is a silent announcement but shouts that the Creator God has been at work and still maintains the world.

And so, in his letter to the Romans, Paul writes:

> But I say, surely they have never heard, have they?
> On the contrary:
> "THEIR VOICE HAS GONE OUT INTO ALL THE EARTH,
> AND THEIR WORDS TO THE ENDS OF THE WORLD."
> (Romans 10:18 NASB)

He quotes from Psalm 19:4. The voices come from God's silent handiwork. Paul is confident that the glory of God speaks in a way that does not necessarily speak in human words or concepts but silently shouts that there is a Creator whose handiwork should wake them up to reality.

As we stand with Jesus in this garden space today, he affirms that he has always lit the way for every human. Today, he is here for you in particular. He brings wisdom, not in principles but in person. Following him develops discernment, makes you whole with no regret, and protects you from stumbling into harm—he is your light in the dark.

He says, "*I will always be bright in your dark, walk with you, and nudge your heart to paths of contentment and wonder. Do not look to find Me in the beauty of the world.*

"*Let what surrounds you point you to Me to bring a proper focus. I am the center of attention because you have access to and enjoyment of everything in Me. I intend only your freedom to find wonder in the universe's macrocosm, and contentment in the microcosm of your heart made whole. Walk with Me; I will light the way.*"

Visions of Paradise

This sundial catches the light of the circling sun to show you where you are in time. The Torah dials us in to living in grace in light of God's rescue. He says, "I carried you on eagles' wings and brought you to myself." So, the eagle wings confirm the gracious act of God that invites faithful response from us. The light of the sun and scripture both light our way to know God and ourselves as known and loved.

Along the Garden Path

This psalm takes us back to the creation of the earth, echoing Genesis 1–3. Imagine standing with God as the first night and day are separated. Each day makes room for the subsequent development to wonder at God's orderly care for us.

Finally, enter the Garden of Eden, where the Tree of Life symbolizes God's care. In Psalm 19, the tree image switches to the Torah (the law) as the

Provision of God (not seen as a set of rules). In both cases, God creates the means to thrive in life.

This psalm honestly acknowledges that we share Adam's and Eve's loss of hearing, sight, and knowledge. God comes to cleanse us from our losses and darkness. He restores connection in our hearts.

Looking at the heavens does not tell us what God is like. Instead, they point to a reality beyond themselves. It is all God's personal, meaningful work.

The world's wonders do not reveal the hidden God but draw attention to reality—the ordered harmony that frames our existence and has something to tell us.

This psalm is truth on tour, announcing there is an Artist who makes good art. We stand within his work, sustained by the splendor of his creation.

The celestial servants have no speech; they are visible voices. They are beheld, not heard. They evoke a curiosity to explore their astonishing magnitudes and minute details.

The sun takes center stage as we walk the path of this psalm. It runs its course and covers the whole earth. Its warmth illuminates everyone, making us sensitive enough to hear the gift of God's grace. The Glory of God is awakened in our senses as the testimony of the good creation points to the Sustainer of it all.

The inaudible cathedral of the cosmos directs us to God's instructive map for life together—the Torah. It is a guide to walking forward with him toward wholeness.

When the Torah is seen as the light of God's love, it becomes a rare treasure. It is better than the pot of gold at the end of a rainbow. It is joy, eating from the Tree of Life for daily connection and conversation with the One who sustains it all.

The psalm closes with a concern over the lingering threat of going astray. The desire to be cleaned of guilt, purged of destructive motives, and redirected from wrongly taken paths is poured out, leaving a yearning for wholeness.

Many things intrude on our lives as addictions. Addictions are part of the human condition. Reeling from what derails our lives, we cover over the pain and loss with temporary fixes, including sex, drugs, and music. The Law brings freedom from enslavement to addictions.

It connects us to the One who can release us. Personal relations are the real thing that nourishes our souls.

The closing prayer asks God to strengthen us again, as He has been doing from the beginning of the world. It requests that God hold our hearts, attune us to His Torah vision, and restore His loving union.

You are standing in a special place. In whatever state your heart may be, you are positioned to be restored by this psalm of wonder to make you a child again.

Indwelling the Garden

Open your ears and eyes to soak in the singing silence.

1 The heavens tell of the glory of God;
And their expanse declares the work of His hands.

Sun and stars still sing the song,
With joyous breath, exhaling long,
Composing mountains, meadows, ponds—
The Creator's symphony invites the throngs.

2 Day to day pours forth speech,
And night to night reveals knowledge.

From dim of dawn to dark of dusk,
Swells the spectrum of light robust,
Spinning melodies through night's dark husk,
Recalling the joy birthed from dust.

3 There is no speech, nor are there words;
Their voice is not heard.

The silent shouts of rocks still play,
A soundless sky forms loud displays,
Dancing trees without voice say,
"Earthmaker bids us to gladly pray."

4 Their line has gone out into all the earth,
And their words to the end of the world.
In them He has placed a tent for the sun,

Under the span of blue above,
Come winged waves of wandering doves,
Whispering out refrains of love,
As the sun caresses the earth like a glove.

5 Which is like a groom coming out of his chamber;
It rejoices like a strong person to run his course.

This faithful fiancé courts the land,
Embarking to join his beloved's hand,
Enlightened earth with his strength expands,
Finishing the day with glory grand.

6 Its rising is from one end of the
heavens,
And its circuit to the other end of
them;
And there is nothing hidden from its
heat.

His course is set to run this race,
Daily keeping his steady pace,
Pouring out a warming grace,
No shadow is found upon his face.

7 The Law of the LORD is perfect,
restoring the soul;
The testimony of the LORD is sure,
making wise the simple.

God's true voice will guide life's roam,
His steadfast ways will build each
home.
A leading light through the unknown,
So innocent hearts will find His
throne.

8 The precepts of the LORD are right,
rejoicing the heart;
The commandment of the LORD is
pure, enlightening the eyes.

Compel me deep within my soul,
To spark an urge to reach Your
goal.
Your wisdom heals my heart to whole,
Brightly shining on our earthly
stroll.

9 The fear of the LORD is clean,
enduring forever;
The judgments of the LORD are true;
they are righteous altogether.

Reverence burns from deep within;
I feel the source where souls begin.
The Spirit's fruit grows through
discipline,
Your truth is my breath's origin.

10 They are more desirable than gold,
yes, than much pure gold;
Sweeter also than honey and
drippings of the honeycomb.

Each word You speak is sweet to taste,
All treasure is in You encased.
No purer pleasure can be chased
Than to find my heart in You
embraced.

11 Moreover, Your servant is warned
by them;
In keeping them there is great
reward.

Caution steers one from the blow
Of chaos, wrecking lives below.
Redirected to build trust slow,
Becoming strong in joy's afterglow.

[12] Who can discern *his* errors? Acquit me of hidden *faults*.

Blind, I wander, without Your Wind,
You heal me from the ways I've sinned.
Please cover me, my faults rescind;
Release me from the pain lies spin.

[13] Also keep Your servant back from presumptuous *sins*;
Let them not rule over me;
Then I will be innocent,
And I will be blameless of great wrongdoing.

Protect me from my pompous plans,
Foolhardy stunts, my whole life's span.
When I forget love's gracious bans,
Please pardon me; let Your grace expand.

[14] May the words of my mouth and the meditation of my heart
Be acceptable in Your sight,
LORD, my rock and my Redeemer.

From deep within, I speak out bold,
Contemplating Your story told.
May joy fill Your eyes as You behold
Your humble child, oh Friend of old.

Taking Reflections with You

I hope you feel a humble delight as you savor your smallness in light of the greatness of the One who cares for you.

- This psalm is full of images to spark the imagination. Did *specific words* open a vista newly encountered that ignited new emotions?
- How did God's grandeur impact you in this psalm? Did you find the words about God's Torah, provision, and presence helped you to see God in a new way?
- Did you hear the silent voices of creation pointing to the One who does speak in his Torah-way? Did you see *who you are* as one who is cared for, opening to curiosity about what God has made possible?
- How did you feel about your *relationship with* God as this magnificent psalm ended? Can you sense his embrace, al-

ways making a way for you to be cleansed and included by him?

- Can you see Jesus looking at you with wonder and delight, enjoying what you are doing with your gifted life, and telling you so in his own words? Let him.
- What wonder was awakened in the psalm to be a curious child again, wanting to ask a question? What would you like to ask?

Final Embrace

This robust psalm is an invitation to open to the whole world. Read it like a child on a summer's night, seeing the last of the setting sun crimson on the horizon, shooting stars in momentary blaze, and the constant wonder of the universe. Add a goblet of your favorite drink and a crackling fire. Let wonder lead your imagination to the grandeur of it all and the embrace of the One who made it and you to be held dearly.

Celestial art.
Your part.
From the start.
Handiwork's spark.
Day after day.
Night's ensuing display.
Creation at play.
With one thing to say.
"He made us this way."
Visual voices.
Vibrant and viral.
Daily vigil.
Veiling and unveiling.
Pavilioned and parading.
Lighting and warming.
The heavens performing.
The Way.
Repairing.
Reviving.
Wisdom guiding.
Energizing.
Radiance supersizing.
Motivated.
Illuminated.
Attitude elated.
Aligned as created.
Going for pure Gold.
Sweetness to behold.
My heart You hold.
Returned.
Tree of Life.
Shedding the strife.
Cleansing.
Acquitting.
With You, I am sitting.
Mouth filled with light.
Heart flowing bright.
Pleased and pleasing.

Psalm 20

Prayer for Peace

Some trust in chariots and some in horses,
but we trust in the name of the LORD *our God.*
(Psalm 20:7 NIV)

Surveying the Garden

Bracing may exceed our ability for embracing.

"I am afraid of what will happen if . . ." is the lead-in line of our lives that stops us. It is our creed, our deepest belief. So, we brace to protect ourselves.

Getting ready for challenges can become our life's work. If so, our attitude entering the Garden of Life will be full of emotional resistance.

We may face challenges with family, work, money, neighbors—the list goes on. Our groan may be small, but it is felt deeply.

We easily get stuck in our resistant stances. We may feel trapped, followed by waves of anxiety.

Our lives may feel like we need a big break—or an answer to our prayers. Life may seem out of control. We may be battling age, lack of adequate resources, or being different. Our garden of contentment appears overgrown and unruly.

King David was a man after God's own heart, but plenty of people were after his head. Plus, he had internal struggles to deal with.

This psalm invites us into his prayer time to ask for our well-being as the mystery of our lives. It creates a space for us to join in, depending on the wisdom and faithfulness of God, one day at a time.

Our lives are unfinished, which can leave us feeling unsettled. We need to know what courage looks like. When focused on ourselves, our anxiety can easily distract us.

We need contentment. That serene place comes when we expect nothing, trusting that God will make a way to bring us through.

Jesus's name means "God saves, rescues, or makes alive." He invites you to say his name and let it simply speak to your heart, "I am Jesus; I am here to release you into life with Me. Let go of trying to manage it all by yourself."

Into the Garden with God

Sometimes, the garden of life is heavy with the weight of responsibility. We feel overwhelmed by the struggles. Some parts seem impossible, like living on an emotional battlefield.

Sometimes, we know what is missing. Other times, we are just exhausted. We would cry out for help if we thought someone cared. We live in the shadow of not knowing how to proceed. Weightiness grinds us to a stop.

Paul felt this burden but also found a resolve. In Philippians, he came to a settled, trusting place and said:

> **I know how to get along with little, and I also know how to live in prosperity; in any and every circumstance I have learned the secret of being filled and going hungry, both of having abundance and suffering need. [13] I can do all things through Him who strengthens me.**
>
> (Philippians 4:12–13 NASB)

His resilience was not a matter of learning strategies or having adequate resources. He knew he was not alone.

Paul's secret was in having the right partner to share his struggles. He knew Jesus was the One who would get him through. Victory was found in giving the outcome to the One who makes good out of all things.

On a banner day, we lift a flag of triumph, making it through the tough days and being unstoppable. *Jesus lifts that banner for you, and it says "Shalom," which can be peace, or designate that place of emotional conquest as Jesus says, "My grace will rain down on you. We will gather on the other side of this and taste victory together." It will be a banner day.*

Visions of Paradise

Your banner celebrates peace with God. It waves to all whom you know and love. It reminds you of all who have died, who are living, and who you hope will inherit a peaceful world. Banners dance in the wind, moved by the Other, who breathes life into you.

Along the Garden Path

Lest we forget, we set reminders.

We all have days and nights when distress floods everything, and we feel paralyzed.

We want a way forward. We desire solutions from someone capable of seeing what we cannot. We hope for wisdom from the very heart of God, his sanctuary of security. We want his stabilizing insight to sustain us another day.

We fondly recall the days gone by. We felt the blessings. A divine, pleasurable pause nourished us, now providing a seed of hope. We are mindful of the fact that God never forgets us. He even cares for the birds of the field. We know that we are held in his heart.

As we wait on him, we discover he has already gone before us. The sound of his voice ignites our hearts to resound with gratitude.

Jesus lifts a flag to celebrate the joy of peace, his peace—a true *shalom* that unfurls in us courage and bravery to face another day.

In his presence, the day's conflicts fade. You are part of his covenant community, embraced within his life. Gathered together, you respond to the promise that is constantly being answered. The Anointed Messiah, whose name is Jesus, has come from heaven with a hand reached out to save. He is near.

The hand that made you will also save you. Some people trust in technology, the stock market, the government, or a grand dream. But wise persons trust in being a child of this One we are proud to call our Friend and God.

We rise to face another day with gratitude. We find courage in knowing that he answered our call. We are going forward together.

Victory comes in being included in a circle of love with the capacity to love unconditionally. He is patiently waiting for you to answer. Remember, lest we forget.

Indwelling the Garden

1 May the LORD answer you on a day of trouble!
May the name of the God of Jacob protect you!

Anguish wraps me, bound complete,
I need Your sure release.
Please, unbind my shackled feet,
Secure my coming peace.

2 May He send you help from the sanctuary,
And support you from Zion!

Come running from Your dwelling place,
To grasp my outstretched hand.
Release Your flowing, giving grace,
Beside me, now come stand.

3 May He remember all your meal offerings
And accept your burnt offering! [Selah]

Recollect the journeys here,
A pilgrimage of praise.
Accept my joyful love made clear,
As prayerful gifts I raise.
[I rest in You]

4 May He grant you your heart's desire
And fulfill your whole plan!

My deepest yearnings now fulfill,
Walking by Your side.
Your love will lead by waters still,
In Your steps, I will abide.

5 We will sing for joy over your victory,
And in the name of our God we will set up our banners.
May the LORD fulfill all your desires.

Strum the harp and lift the song,
With flowing joy, we celebrate.
For Your peaceful tent, we long,
As hope inquires at Your gates.

6 Now I know that the LORD saves His anointed;
He will answer him from His holy heaven
With the saving strength of His right hand.

When desperate days seemed dismally drear,
The clouds began to part,
Made serene, as You came near,
You calmed my weary heart.

7 Some *praise their* chariots and some *their* horses,
But we will praise the name of the LORD, our God.

Some seem secure in self-made strength,
Their castles briefly stand.
But trusting You, my life's full length,
I dwell within Your hands.

8 They have bowed down and fallen,
But we have risen and stood upright.

Power-hungry, they dug their grave,
Which opened before their eyes.
But by Your victory, we are saved,
From death we will surely rise.

9 Save, LORD;
May the King answer us on the day we call.

Now, we savor security,
Your fulfilling, embracing relief.
Feed us love's maturity,
Supply sap for this shaking leaf.

Taking Reflections with You

- What words resonated in your heart that echo with this psalm's key phrases as you read?
- How did the presence of God's ultimate peace help you to see God in a new way?
- Did this psalm help you hear any hidden cries in your heart? What are you discovering about *who you are*, recognizing what gives you deep security, and what is revealed about something important that may be missing?
- What is the state of your *relationship with God* around the issue of shalom? Is this kind of peace one you feel being given to you in your relationship with God? What is your physical posture when accepting shalom?
- Can you hear *Jesus speaking shalom* into your life situations? What is he saying?
- What can you *put into a sentence to express* where you need peace and where you have been trying to find it?

Final Embrace

How is your heart at trusting? Is your heart like cut flowers, with short seasons of fading color? Or is your heart flourishing with constant feeding, pruning, and enjoyment like a living plant?

Battlefield.
Need to be healed.
Pain unreal.
Scars revealed.
Answers.
Responses.
Solutions.
Insufficient conclusions.
Needing resolutions.
Thirsty for love's infusion.
Enough seclusion.
From above.
Send Your Dove.
Lift me with love.
Mindful.
Delightful.
Eventful.
Reciprocal.
Beyond the lull.
Rise.

Rest.
Relief.
Release.
Relish the moment.
Hope's atonement.
Joy's bestowment.
Heart's true enrollment.
Resounding enjoyment.
Love's full employment.
No more postponement.
Unfurling with freedom's
endowment.
Banner day.
I hear You say.
Trust and obey.
Don't turn away.
With Me stay.
Rise and play.
Child of the King.
Sing.

Psalm 21

Royal Covenant Celebration

For the king trusts in the Lord*;*
through the unfailing love of the Most High he will not be shaken.
(Psalm 21:7 NIV)

Surveying the Garden

What we celebrate defines us.

While this psalm celebrates the King's gratitude for provision and protection, it invites us beyond that viewpoint.

This psalm reflects past blessings and the hope of being present with God in the future. Mostly, it celebrates face-to-face connection. This posture focuses on a loyal love that stirs the heart to embrace another day together.

People daily choose lesser loyalties in life. Many are obsessed with their security. They disconnect from neighbors and reduce their world to their bubble. Since God feels like an interruption, they dismiss him as a fairy tale. Celebrating their separate space becomes the point, imagining an artificial freedom from others. They miss the authentic freedom of shared life, loving and being loved.

Today, we celebrate leadership that makes us appreciate God's faithfulness in the past and intimacy in the present. God raises kings and queens, and other leaders, calling them to be servants of God and the people.

This servant leadership creates a space for a covenant community—people who celebrate their life's story together. Leadership focuses on bringing people together, affirming connections and friendships, and remembering what is important as they gather to embrace the road ahead with courage.

Jesus invites you into this space to remember that:

- He is *the King* who gives all.
- He became a Resurrected *Priest*, celebrating the union and communion of God and humanity.
- He is a *Prophet* who reveals the gracious intentions of God.

Jesus stands against what fractures us to fulfill God's gathering and caring. He is the center of today's celebration; its meaning all points to him.

Jesus throws a royal robe around you and invites you to join the celebration, saying, "Come, royal child, for you are a child of the King. Come to the throne of my Father's compassion and find release and peace to remember who you are and whose you are. Your seat is close to the front; you are seen and beloved in this place."

Into the Garden with God

Jesus was a king and still is the King. But he came as a servant.

Jesus never sought to be like the kings of this earth. He came to bring love, the driving force of the kingdom of God.

Jesus does not set up armies and collect taxes. He gathers the dispersed of the earth to come into his garden to share the beauty and abundance of his Father's welcoming presence.

This part of the garden has been prepared for a long time. Jesus, as the King, has been waiting for you. He pointed to this when he said,

> **"Then the King will say to those on His right, 'Come, you who are blessed of My Father, inherit the kingdom prepared for you from the foundation of the world.'"**
> (Matthew 25:34 NASB)

This invitation refers to the gathering celebration that is the fruit of his mission.

This psalm points us to the fulfillment of all Jesus came for. You are leaning into his promised future. You are being reminded that you are a citizen of this kingdom, a child of this family—all as a pure gift.

You are entering the Crown Garden and sense the royal surroundings. It is adorned with honor and memory. The setting draws your attention to the King, who is the Gardener. He fills the majestic location. But also notice his pruning shears and watering can, shovel, and wheelbarrow, and recycling bins to meet every circumstance—he wears work clothes as the Tending King.

Visions of Paradise

This part of the garden, with its throne, crown, and royal décor, gives you a sense of delightful decency. It is not stuffy or artificial. It is made freeing by the evident attentiveness of the King to create enjoyment and gathering. It is joy in regal blooming.

Along the Garden Path

This psalm is a prayerful path into the presence of the King. The air is light with gratitude that sparkles from excited conversations as you walk by. They all have a sense of satisfied delight.

This King rules all seasons of life. You feel the crispness of winter, the opening profusion of spring, the peaceful pause of summer, and the cornucopia of autumn all in the same sweeping glance. He fulfills our heart's desire in the rhythms of life. Nothing has been withheld.

A royal goblet of blessing is offered to you. You feel bathed in the golden light of the moment as you go to meet the King.

You sense an enduring bounty that stretches on in this place. Time flows like a graceful river, drawing you to the face of the One waiting for you to immerse you within his glorious, restoring embrace.

Your heart leaps with the joy of his presence, basking in this moment of blessing. This blessing echoes back to the promise to Abraham, through whom all the families of the earth are blessed. This moment is a victorious echo of that vow.

The covenanting promise to care for his family envelops this moment. Loving-kindness holds you firm. Your future feels bright as you celebrate his victories over life's battles.

This King has the power to comfort the oppressed and to trouble the comfortable who have lost sensitivity to others. Where the radiance of his face has been a delight to you, it becomes a refining fire to those whose selfish greed consumes others.

Now, a circle is formed. Hand in hand, a dance celebrates the strength and power of the King with a crowning circle of singing.

These blessed people share the delight of their proximity to the King. All together, they sing his name with grateful hearts. Each person knows they are uniquely known. Yet, they also recognize they belong together in the oneness of being held as beloved.

This crowd is the crown of the King of the Cosmos. All have come to confirm that his love has birthed a loyal love in them that makes this garden their home with him.

You are beloved by a King who calls you His child. He beckons you to come and drink what he calls the Water of Life. It is better than wine and makes you feel alive like never before. It cleanses and clarifies who you are as you drink this freeing cup of love.

Indwelling the Garden

1 Lord, in Your strength the king will
be glad,
And in Your salvation how greatly he
will rejoice!

2 You have given him his heart's
desire,
And You have not withheld the
request of his lips. [Selah]

3 For You meet him with the blessings
of good things;
You set a crown of pure gold on his
head.

4 He asked for life from You,
You gave it to him,
Length of days forever and ever.

5 His glory is great through Your
salvation,
Splendor and majesty You place upon
him.

6 For You make him most blessed
forever;
You make him joyful with the joy of
Your presence.

Courage is born without delay
From trusting now that You will stay.
My jubilance joins with justice full,
Drawn to where Your pleasure pulls.

Fondness deep has filled my air,
Breathed so free, with tender care,
I uttered a wish; You swift replied,
You knew my heart and heard my cry.
[I rest in You]

Abundance streams from Your goodwill,
My unknown needs You fulsome fill.
Honor crowns my head with peace,
Surrounded safe, my worries cease.

Winding down the corridors of time,
Extending grace and pleasures fine,
You lead me on to eternity's door,
Glimpsing all that's kept in store.

You sheltered me with due regard,
You raised me up when days were hard.
To lofty places I now go,
Because You lift me from here below.

I'm full beyond my wildest dreams,
Behind me fades my human schemes.
Enjoyment brims my spirit's song,
Beside You now, where I belong.

7 For the king trusts in the LORD,
And through the faithfulness of the
Most High he will not be shaken.

Confidence soars in me complete,
Soaked in Your richness, all replete.
Profuse loving is Your attire,
Fearlessly fulfilling my hope's desire.

8 Your hand will find all Your
enemies;
Your right hand will find those who
hate You.

Your careful hand will form a fence,
Resisting foes, You're my sure
defense.
Your securing touch will keep me safe,
Withstanding those who against
You chafe.

9 You will make them as a fiery oven
in the time of Your anger;
The LORD will swallow them up in his
wrath,
And fire will devour them.

Your refining fire is just to the end,
Your purity corrects as love
descends,
Your light floods shadows, where lives
decay,
Your radiant love consumes the day.

10 You will eliminate their descendants from the earth,
And their children from among the
sons of mankind.

Waves of destruction by You are
bound,
Against Your storm wall, they will
pound.
Unchecked currents, You will tame,
Ravaged shorelines, You will
reclaim.

11 Though they intended evil against
You
And devised a plot,
They will not succeed.

Scheming plans of malicious men
You surely bring to naught again.
They stretch to take what is not
theirs,
You quench their wildfires as they
flare.

12 For You will make them turn their
back;
You will take aim at their faces with
Your bowstrings.

When their attack is fully unleashed
You stop them where their war has
reached,
While they shake a defiant fist,
Like the rising sun, You dispel their
mist.

13 Be exalted, LORD, in Your strength;
We will sing and praise Your power.

Sweet Adoration, we lift to You!
Whispering a breath of what is due.
With a chorus joined by the world around,
Our gratitude echoes Your heartbeat's sound.

Taking Reflections with You

Slow down from the protection, dance, and the festivity. Let the gratitude wash through you like fresh, cold water.

- Think back on the psalm and listen *for words* that awaken new emotions from sitting with royalty who loves you.
- How did God show up for you? Did your internal thoughts and feelings churn up something that allowed you to see God differently?
- How did this psalm help you to remember how you have been blessed? What do you take for granted, and what could you not live without? How do these discerning thoughts help you to see *who you are*?
- Did you resonate with the celebration in this psalm as being true to your *relationship with* God? Do you have a new vision of yourself as a child of the King?
- What is the King *saying today* in the face of what threatens you?
- What *words do you use* to adore the King when celebrating his provision and presence?

Final Embrace

A life of festivity leaves you full of grateful memories. The moments spent in embracing the good with people, laughing and sharing stories, or stopping for moments of sweet solitude, are priceless. Revisiting the moments that were rich enough to still come to mind is a new form of theater in mindful refreshment. As you read slowly, see what flashes across the screen of your mind.

Celebration.
Life's destination.
Without reservation.
Joy's fullest invitation.
The King has come.
Love pays attention.
Even with human rejection.
Crucifixion.
Resurrection.
Ascension.
Freedom's flowing reflection.
Community connection.
Fullest satisfaction.
Heart's desire.
Mind inspired.
A life not to be retired.
Soul on fire.
Sipping immensity, freely acquired.
Singing with a holy choir.
Only grace required.
Sparkling.
Beauty.
Bounty.
Encountering reality.
The gold of glory.
The deepest story.
Splendor.
Majesty.
Victory.
With.
Just.
You.
And Me.

Psalm 22

Lament for the Love of the World

But you, LORD, do not be far from me.
You are my strength; come quickly to help me.
(Psalm 22:19 NIV)

Surveying the Garden

Have you ever felt dehumanized?

The experience may include being belittled, excluded, abandoned, silenced, lied about, or becoming invisible.

Our inhumanity is a raw wound that may never heal. But with honest acknowledgment, one can begin regaining holy ground, a time and place to be made whole. That process never happens alone.

We need a First Responder to tend to the tenderest places in us, to help in our pain, lament over what has been lost and still aches, and help to heal by releasing in silence, weeping, or finding honor.

This psalm's part of the garden includes the greenhouse, where the promise of what is yet to come brings hope. There is a mulching bin of autumn leaf piles with the worms already at work in the cycles of death and new life.

A greenhouse is an enclosed space that keeps out what damages. At the same time, it nurtures what is possible for new growth. Decay and saved seeds become the future's hope with the promise of beauty.

Jesus knew the whole psalm. Years of praying it made him profoundly aware of its loss and hope. And on that night, on the Cross, he repeated its first line, it came with its punctuation of pain: "My God, my God, why have you forsaken me?" Imagine feeling with him as you read. Even there, hope was already in sight in that shadowy night, as you will see at the end of this psalm.

Feel the depth of despair and distance at the start. In the horror of that night, hear those agonized words roar across the landscape for all the world.

Jesus did not want an answer as to *why* he was in this state. He needed no explanation. By crying out "My God," he confessed an intimacy and faith, not appealing to "the Man upstairs," but to the only One Person who could bear with him through his pain. These words split the night to reveal his deepest yearning for his Father's presence.

The final part of this psalm was the ultimate punctuation of praise in the pleasure of God's presence. In the end, love was the reason he could say, "It is finished." His Father's mission was complete.

With eyes of love, Jesus looks at you and says, "I will be with you in paradise today, here in this garden. I will tell you the story of My love and how it extends from humble worms to building My kingdom. I make beautiful things out of mud. Come learn of My love in the greenhouse of your soul."

Into the Garden with God

This psalm connects us to the story of Jesus. From the beginning, the desperate words accentuate this zenith of his life—the Cross. We can easily miss the invitation to hope for humanity set in motion that day.

In this psalm, we enter a place confronted by dying and rising. Jesus knew that his life would not be one of a popular teacher, appreciated for what he had to offer. He offered hope and the restoration of humanity in relationship with his Father. Not everyone wanted this gift.

Jesus did not come to shame us or tell us bad news. He came to tell us what was actually going on. He proclaimed the kingdom of God and invited us to his garden, a place of shared fruitfulness.

An empty greenhouse can look rather stark and lifeless. It takes a gardener to tell you what preparations can do and glimpse the abundance of coming beauty. The Cross is a similar mystery.

Every season of loss and pain has an end. With the proper companions, it can be the beginning of seasons of splendor. There will be other seasons of survival. Do not go it alone; this process develops something significant in you—a fruitful heart.

Paul knows about these changing seasons and rhythms. He knows there will be seasons of pain and shame, but this greenhouse has a Master Gardener who guides him toward a richer hope. Paul tells his Roman friends,

And hope does not disappoint, because the love of God has been poured out within our hearts through the Holy Spirit who was given to us.
(Romans 5:5 NASB)

Paul and Jesus loved this greenhouse of a psalm because it was so brutally honest and strikingly hopeful. It is not just another praise hymn; it has blues and rhapsody wrapped in soul-wrenching wonder to expand our capacity to hear God's heart deeply.

Entering a greenhouse, we step into a processing place. It is ever-changing and always has the same task—to grow new life. Jesus gets his hands dirty in his greenhouse. He encourages us to go with him to this place to discover what will be—and what we can be.

Jesus has a vivid sense of growth and what is happening "now and not yet" in your life. He knows what blossoms and bears fruit; he lived his human life and sent his cultivating Spirit. You are in good hands.

Jesus's releasing, visionary words draw you forward, "Come and die to that past that was all about you and become new within My care."

Visions of Paradise

In this greenhouse, you will feel the air. It holds a mixture of decaying compost from the past and, at the same time, is fragrant with a sense of preparation for growth and new life. The air is heavy with possibility. It awakens what is dead. It is a caring place designed to sprout new life in you.

Along the Garden Path

This garden path toward the greenhouse has some dark shadows.

You know Jesus is beside you, yet the shadows distract you. Sidetracked from him, you may feel suddenly alone.

At times, you may have felt abandoned by those who should have been there for you.

Today, you are standing on holy ground. It is not holy with brilliance; it is holy in that God meets you there. In your deepest darkness, he understands your heart.

Glancing up, you realize that the shadows are so dark because of the intense light that comes through the foliage along the path.

You feel the Spirit's presence return. He reminds you of the Cross so long ago; it still speaks to you now. The Spirit lets you hear the bellowing roar of Jesus as he suffers in an hour of abuse by his accusers.

Still, the agony of abandonment echoes in all who weep in the night. There is no peace in that place. But you also are given ears to listen to his heart: "For the love of you, I left my Father's side to bring you home. I am loving you to death and to life again." A light shines in the darkness.

Jesus, the embodiment of grace, willingly endured disgrace to redeem us through his grace. The shame of Adam and Eve covered this naked bag of bones. The hostility of humanity battered his every fiber.

More amazing, those who looked on to this tragedy mocked. The little bit of power they assumed in their superiority bore the stains of all the prejudices humans leave as a mark on those who are different. Imagine the relief for those who shook their heads and poked fun at this powerless One. They did not need to listen to him anymore. It was a tragic kind of release.

We never stand alone. From the day we are born, we are met by the God who weaved us in our mother's womb. He is there as a midwife to spark that first breath, not unlike the breath into Adam in the garden.

We are cared for by family, but he is ever present as the custodian of daily life, cuddling and caressing us with love, disciplining us as we grow, and ever creative in helping us find the gift we may be for others.

Hopefully, we will wake up one day and say, "Oh, You were there all along!" We want to know every day that he is near. He has removed us from darkness to bring us to the light of the kingdom.

Still, there are so many distractions! We hear such violent voices on television. We inch toward defensiveness from a rude encounter, a honking horn, a nasty glance, or another day of exhaustion. We have nothing left to give. And everyone seems to want to take from us, but we are drained.

Our bodies speak to us of the turmoil. Our bones ache. Our shoulders get tight with stress. Our minds get dull and forgetful or just overwhelmed. The courage that once propelled us to jet out the door has withered.

In desperation, you cry out, "Be my help, Lord! Hurry up! I don't know how much longer I can hold on in this pain!" We know we have one precious life to live. It feels like it is slipping away.

And so the resurrection moment comes. Jesus awakens you to a new morning. You suddenly become aware that you are surrounded by others who are brothers and sisters in the family of God. They know how to be together, attentive, caring, and sharing of songs of gratitude and compassion. Having been gifted by God, they bear the fruit of generosity, kindness, speaking, and touching.

Together, these people represent the full spectrum of God's blessings, coming in diverse shapes and sizes, like a botanical garden of backgrounds. The voice of the Resurrected One harmonizes with the many, making this place a holy mosaic of peace for a new era.

The buried seeds that have endowed this place with hope go back centuries to those upon whom the light has come. The Spirit has shone on these underdogs, the outcast, the lonely, all those who sing the song of the afflicted. The Living God has turned their darkness into a deep spiritual, sung in the sunlight.

In this greenhouse, there is always a place to eat. The bread that is served here brings peace to the broken. The wine that is poured celebrates the joy of the kingdom.

In the center of the greenhouse is the Tree of Life. Its fruit is for the healing of the nations and to bless all the earth and all peoples. Hearts are made whole here; all races, generations, genders, social classes, and every other segment we experience are made one new person as they stand before the king.

The sound of many languages colors this place. It is lovely to hear children's voices laughing and older people saying farewells that can only come from knowing there is more to come.

In this place, there is more than enough for everyone. Jesus has called beyond these walls to summon all to this space. It even extends back in time to those who sleep in the earth. It extends to the poor and the well-to-do. It is an inviting table.

The One who died was buried in the ground and rose again; he has gone on before us. He will be with his children as he planned all along. It is completed, but that is not an ending; he brings the beginning of God's shalom—the regaining of peace in relationships because God has brought it to pass and keeps his promised presence alive.

This path has led us on quite the walk from dark to bright daylight, but you are ready to enter all unfolding in this place.

Indwelling the Garden

1 My God, my God, why have You
forsaken me?
Far from my help are the words of my
groaning.

Oh, Love, Oh Love, hope from above,
I feel so desperately lost.
My anguish flows like drops of blood
Sacrificed at the ultimate cost.

2 My God, I cry out by day, but You do
not answer;
And by night, but I have no rest.

Dear Source of Life, all night I wail,
Yet silence wraps my day.
As the sun slowly sinks her sail,
I, in the darkness, lay.

3 Yet You are holy,
You who are enthroned upon the
praises of Israel.

Still, You are my all in all,
The life that breathes my wind,
Reigning tall while kingdoms fall,
Your acclaim is my glorious hymn

4 In You our fathers trusted;
They trusted and You rescued them.

A flood of fathers went before,
Leaning on Your hand.
Believing You would give them more,
You led them to that land.

5 To You they cried out and they fled
to safety;
In You they trusted and were not
disappointed.

When trouble tamed their beating
hearts,
Your courage gave them wings.
You asked them each to play their parts
Through them, Your victory sings.

6 But I am a worm and not a person,
A disgrace of mankind and despised
by the people.

But deep within, I feel defeat,
A carcass hung to dry,
Lamenting the loss of longing love,
Spit on by passersby.

7 All who see me deride me;
They sneer, they shake their heads,
saying,

Unkind words batter my ears,
The pain sinks deep inside.
Satisfied smirks from dark souls lurk,
I want to run and hide.

8 "Turn *him* over to the LORD; let Him
save him;
Let Him rescue him, because He
delights in him."

I reach to You, last Hope of Help,
My breath, revive once more.
Deliver me from the beating blows,
That I might be restored.

9 Yet You are He who brought me
forth from the womb;
You made me trust *when* upon my
mother's breasts.

You sculpted me in soft entomb,
Birthed with a squall of sound,
Suckling then sweet mother's gifts,
Your provisions were all around.

10 I was cast upon You from birth;
You have been my God from my
mother's womb.

Ever cradled in Your arms,
Across the spectrum of my life,
You, so sure, have been my help
Through seasons full of strife.

11 Do not be far from me, for trouble is
near;
For there is no one to help.

Be close this night of harsh defeat,
While others have walked away.
An empty echo fills my soul,
As my life urge fades to gray.

12 Many bulls have surrounded me;
Strong bulls of Bashan have encircled
me.

Ruffians wild, with nostrils wide,
Circle around my feet.
Dancing their triumph to a deafening
pitch,
Gleeful of my sure defeat.

13 They open their mouths wide at me,
As a ravening and roaring lion.

Laughing loud, their heads rolled back,
Jeering at their powerless prey,
Consumed with their haughty hunt for
flesh,
Now stretched out for display.

14 I am poured out like water,
And all my bones are out of joint;
My heart is like wax;
It is melted within me.

I am drained, decanted like the rain,
'Til only last drops remain,
My heart's been attacked like molten wax,
Lost to the flickering flame.

15 My strength is dried up like a piece of pottery,
And my tongue clings to my jaws;
And You lay me in the dust of death.

My lips are gaunt with arid want,
Languishing in the heat,
I cannot speak a single word,
Reduced to dusty defeat.

16 For dogs have surrounded me;
A band of evildoers has encompassed me;
They pierced my hands and my feet.

Scavengers wait to claim their prize,
Hungry in their callous pride,
Puncturing palms and spiking feet,
My dignity fully denied.

17 I can count all my bones.
They look, they stare at me;

My skeleton stretches against my skin,
My carcass cries for relief.
Curious spectators come to look
At my bones, a dying reef.

18 They divide my garments among them,
And they cast lots for my clothing.

What was mine is gone, the dice are rolled,
My belongings they divide.
The simple loot will barely suit,
Who cares, as fate decides?

19 But you, LORD, do not be far away;
You who are my help, hurry to my assistance.

LORD, ever present, hold me now,
Come be here by my side,
May your heart now hear my plea.
Father, be my guide.

20 Save my soul from the sword,
My only life from the power of the dog.

Lead me from this crushing threat,
Ease my tensing fear.
When snipping teeth of doubts dig deep,
Please leash those threats come near.

21 Save me from the lion's mouth;
From the horns of the wild oxen You answer me.

Wild beasts still stalk my life,
Starved, and hungry to devour.
I'm shaken by roars and the horns of boars,
Please, free me in this hour.

22 I will proclaim Your name to my brothers;
In the midst of the assembly I will praise You.

How sweet to be filled by the thought of You,
To recount Your faithful release,
As we gather round and the music sounds,
My kin shall know Your peace.

23 You who fear the LORD, praise Him;
All you descendants of Jacob, glorify Him,
And stand in awe of Him, all you descendants of Israel.

Now all who revere, come near, come near,
The King's arms reach out wide.
This awesome One says come, says come,
Family, come abide.

24 For He has not despised nor scorned the suffering of the afflicted;
Nor has He hidden His face from him;
But when he cried to Him for help, He heard.

When silent, He may seem remote,
But He is never far.
Poor trampled ones, He heartily hears,
His ears are never barred.

25 From You *comes* my praise in the great assembly;
I shall pay my vows before those who fear Him.

You set alight my morning song,
To bless this gathered throng.
A faithful family, focused on You,
Released to worship long.

26 The afflicted will eat and be satisfied;
Those who seek Him will praise the LORD.
May your heart live forever!

All shall come to feast as one,
Nourished by the King,
Pouring out His gifts to all
Around the table ringed.

27 All the ends of the earth
will remember and turn to
the LORD,
And all the families of the nations will worship before You.

Awaken memories of long ago,
Of days in captive lands.
We began to worship then,
Now rapt in adoring stance.

28 For the kingdom is the LORD'S
And He rules over the nations.

The King shall reign, all peoples bow,
He halts all that's in vain,
He brings all people to His care,
Ending earth's fear and pain.

29 All the prosperous of the earth will eat and worship,
All those who go down to the dust will kneel before Him,
Even he who cannot keep his soul alive.

Every shape and every size
Of person will gather 'round.
The intertwining of our lives,
Shall there, at His table, be found.

30 A posterity will serve Him;
It will be told of the Lord to the *coming* generation.

The hope, for those still yet to come,
Lives in His twinkling eye.
We speak about His faithful love,
Good news that finally arrives.

31 They will come and will declare His righteousness
To a people who will be born, that He has performed it.

Shout aloud and sing again,
This never-ending tale,
Of Him who rightly steers all time,
Whose mercy never fails.

Taking Reflections with You

From the Cross to the resurrection, you have just been stretched to unveil the brokenness of humanity and the healing of our personal lives. Reflect and refresh with this, open to restorative joy.

- What *familiar words* in this psalm took on new meaning as you wound through its many images and openings?
- Did you see God in a new way? Could you enter into the experience of Jesus to sense his heart that comes to heal humanity? The opening of pain ends with hope. Did you feel the shift?
- Could you see *who you are* as the object of God's love and restoration in this psalm? Can you sense the kind of plant you are in the greenhouse of possibility?

- When the psalm ended, could you feel a sense of joy in sharing a nurturing *relationship with* God? Did you sense the enduring presence of God when he is silent, discovering he is never far away?
- Could you *hear Jesus's words* from the Cross? Did he address you like he addressed others from the Cross?
- What *words did you want to shout* to Jesus in his hour of pain? What words came at the morning table of feasting?

Final Embrace

This poem takes you into a moment in time when all seemed lost on the Cross. We live in the face of loss, as well as the possibility of resurrection. This trodden path is a wrestling experience that goes to the depths of pain but does not leave you there. Take the journey; you are not alone.

Inhumane.
Teardrop in the rain.
Forgotten.
Abandoned.
The heart so stained with pain.
Silence.
In the midst of violence.
Distance.
So much resistance.
Hushed quiet.
But internally, a riot.
Then I heard Your song.
Love employed.
Peace deployed.
All enjoyed.
Trust on steroids.
But then destroyed.
I am a worm.
Left to squirm.
A sad disgrace.
Unrecognizable face.
Dehumanizing place.
Bloody and debased.
Hostility unlaced.
Hatred's aftertaste.
Sinking into empty space.
Once I was new.
Born with the help of You.
A joyful noise.
A mother's poise.
Before I had toys.
First kiss of joys.
Cuddled in love's arms.
Away from all the harms.
Embraced by all Your charms.
But then.
Trouble came.
You seemed gone.
Love withdrawn.
Surrounded.
Hounded.
Pounded.
Beastliness.
Gaping emptiness.

Twisting brokenness.
Melting formlessness.
Hollowness.
Wordless.
Dust.
Punctured.
Exhausted.
Sniffed.
Poked.
Broken.
Bled.
Boney blob.
Tossed aside.
Hasten . . .
Your aid.
My life.
Lift me from this strife.
I need a turning point.
Glory.
Another chapter of the story.
Return to community.
Praise with all the company.
Filled with generosity.
Finding solidarity.
Exploring love's velocity.
Meal of inclusivity.
Faithful assembly.
Poor and wealthy see.
Love's liberality.
Cheerful we come to eat.
Satisfied we finally leave.
Embracing all we meet.
Announcing the King complete.
In life.
In death.
In sleep.
Awake.
Me.
You.
All posterity.
Wonders see.
Endless bounty.
Shalom means.
It's all.
Complete.

Psalm 23

Cojourners on Life's Journey

Surely your goodness and love will follow me all the
days of my life,
and I will dwell in the house of the Lord *forever.*
(Psalm 23:6 NIV)

Surveying the Garden

Is anything missing from your life?

Stop for a moment and say in your head, "I lack nothing." Say it a few times. Then, ask yourself if you really believe that.

Listen for that voice that says, "Wait a minute! I lack lots of things that would make me happy, like . . ."

We're always on the hunt for more, aren't we?

With these desires laid bare, they reveal a cavernous lack in our daily existence, an emptiness that we recognize as discontent.

Psalm 23 is filled with movement to live with contentment. We are called today by God to be cojourners, meaning travelers together. But we are not equals. We call him the Lord. We are wayfarers with him.

Only God can meet our deep human needs: provision, protection, support, direction, deliverance, and so much more. He desires to satisfy our heart's hunger.

Jesus will invite you to see possibilities for fulfillment and challenge your current expectations.

But we must be clear about one thing. Most of us are not as confident or content as this psalm would like to portray.

This journey will offer us a path to serenity. And on it we will be the Lord's trusting sheep. Ultimately, this pilgrimage will build our resilience and help us know this Shepherd's presence.

We are pilgrims on this garden path, seeking a destination. We pass by inviting pools of refreshment. We encounter life's deficiencies and come close to death's door. Our enemies, or those who have made our lives hard, sometimes family members, are close by. But we go with God. His fierce tenderness, along with the tools he carries, directly defends us on our journey.

There is a table at the end of the trek. We are invited to envision the sweetest communion possible. We are seated at this table with Jesus. He opens the vista that calls forth a thanksgiving hymn. We drink his cup of joy and are crowned with honor only he can bestow.

Jesus stands just inside the entrance to the garden, reaches out his shepherd's crook, and smilingly pulls you inside and says, "I have all we will need here. Let all your pressures and wants drop off your shoulders and be washed out of your mind. Let me be your Host today. I will heal those empty and tired places in you. I will lead you in an exodus from what enslaves you." You are *on your way to the feast of all feasts with the Father and all his family, accompanied by his Son.*

Into the Garden with God

Jesus is the Good Shepherd.

Only he really knows what that means. Observe how he knows everything about our route along the garden today. Notice how he embraces all that life may bring and finds a way through.

Jesus knows how to get you to the tent of meeting. He can lament with you and praise you. He knows the Psalms.

Jesus knows about getting through sickness and restoring health. He has the tender skills and self-sacrificing courage to live up to his name—Immanuel, which means God with us, not you.

Jesus is at home in gardens and vineyards, but also with his sheep. In John 10:2–4, Jesus says:

> "But the one who enters by the door is a shepherd of the
> sheep. [3] To him the doorkeeper opens, and the sheep listen to
> his voice, and he calls his own sheep by name and leads them
> out. [4] When he puts all his own *sheep* outside, he goes ahead of
> them, and the sheep follow him because they know his voice."

And later in John, he says,

> [14] "I am the good shepherd, and I know My own, and My own know me, [15] just as the Father knows Me and I know the Father; and I lay down My life for the sheep."
> (John 10:2–4, 14–15 NASB)

The New Testament does not quote Psalm 23, but Jesus embodies the life to which this psalm points. He is that ever-present Shepherd. He desires us to know God's voice, accompany him, and respond attentively to his care.

The Shepherd is calling you to join him at his high table. His provision and attitude of ultimate care for you are the invitation of a lifetime, not just to be satisfied for a night, but to be in the enlivening presence of the Chief Shepherd who is patting the place next to him as he says, "Come." And you recognize his voice . . .

Visions of Paradise

In the distance, you can still see the valley of the shadow of death. But the welcoming table is what fills your awareness. Even more clearly, you hear the unseen voice that draws you to come and sit. You feel as though everyone has excitedly been waiting for you, but you are overwhelmed by the presence of the Loving Host.

Along the Garden Path

One does not just stumble onto this table. When you discover it, you will find it is always prepared for guests, and you will arrive at its companionable space, which has been waiting for you.

Psalm 22 began with a cry of abandonment in the night: "My God, my God." The path to this psalm begins with "My Shepherd," confessing a life of secure attachment, safe and beloved.

The Shepherd is present and active, sustaining you with personal, intimate camaraderie as a living Lord: the embrace of the God of Love.

As you breathe "My Shepherd," you come to know what it means to know you are known. He is yours only because you were first his.

In this moment, you find yourself saying, "You are more than enough." This affirmation is not about filling a bank account, or a doctor's report of good health. You are experiencing what can only be expressed when we discover grace. This is the fullness of being met, loved, and belonging, like a great symphony's final, resounding chord.

We pass through a mountain meadow. Every year, it dies and rises anew in a cycle of renewal. All living things, including humans, have rhythms of withdrawal and return; these rhythms allow us to appreciate times of connection and endure times of desperation. But we know we are not alone, even though we may feel lonely.

The images of green pastures, resting places, blissful brooks, and clear pools of water speak of having the best that can renew our soul—the heartbeat of life in connection. The joy is in the joining.

When we stray and disconnect, becoming lost sheep and taking treacherous paths, he comes looking for us to restore the vitality of being alive.

The Shepherd has well-worn paths to follow, much like the Torah, which is not a set of rules but is a way to life. He is true to being our Creator, Sustainer, and the One who redeems our life, even when we throw it away. He carries us on his shoulders when we are weary. But he enjoys it when we walk in his pathway for the pure pleasure of being with him.

But the shadows do come. Death is the place on life's route where all other guides—whether family or doctors—must turn back. We must walk it at God's speed. We cannot see well. What we can do is shed our fear that disaster will meet us.

With failing strength, we are only consoled when we know one key thing: He is with us. He is before us, behind us, beside us, and in us. His presence brings confidence. When the Spirit moves in us, we cry out, "Abba, dear Father," finding strength that does not originate in us. We share this journey with Jesus, who brings us to his Father's house of love.

The table is set. It is a Royal Feast. It is well-laid out to feast the eyes just as much as the tongue and the belly. The Host stands welcoming. A seat is prepared just for you. This is a celebratory meal.

Those who have made life difficult are in plain sight. But you can feel the fading away of the need to judge, punish, get back at, and be done with those people. They are not excluded, but they are docile.

You are crowned with love and joy. Oil is the symbol that lets you know the Holy Spirit blesses you, but it also signifies that you are a member of this beloved community of friends who share this fragrant emblem of hospitality.

The food is plentiful and delicious, and the cup is filled to an abundance that fills your heart with gratitude and delight. The chalice of blessing is a foretaste of the kingdom coming. This table reorients you to what is important—not being a stranger, or even a guest—you are a child of this King and you are home.

All along, you were guided by Jesus, but he had companions who followed and watched out for you all the way. Sweet favor and loving-kindness are two faithful attendants who have pursued you all along the way to get you to this place.

But this is not a fixed place; it is an alfresco, open-air table with an embracing presence. You know that, for the rest of your life, you will have the pleasure of living within this surroundedness.

God's presence encircles your life. You do not need to travel far to find him; you only need to have your heart opened. Here is your Father's dwelling, to which you are awakening like a reborn child.

Welcome home and enter into the open spaces made for you to know true freedom.

Indwelling the Garden

1 The LORD is my shepherd,
I will not be in need.

2 He lets me lie down in green
pastures;
He leads me beside quiet waters.

3 He restores my soul;
He guides me in the paths of
righteousness
For the sake of His name.

4 Even though I walk
through the valley of the shadow
of death,
I fear no evil,
for You are with me;
Your rod and Your staff,
they comfort me.

5 You prepare a table before me
in the presence of my enemies;
You have anointed my head with oil;
My cup overflows.

6 Certainly goodness and faithfulness
will follow me all the days of my
life,
And my dwelling *will be* in the house
of the LORD forever.

Contentment supreme in meadow
green,
I live within Your care,
Lacking nothing I may need,
With Your tender heart laid bare.

With restoring rest, my days so blessed,
In Your flowering fields so full,
You calm my chest, revive the best,
Sipping from pools brimful.
You recreate my every morn,
My journey thrilled anew,
As through each day You lead the way,
I securely roam with You

When I near death, I need Your breath
To endure this blackest gorge.
My quaking calms, held by Your arms,
Soothed within love's forge.

Your banquet's well-laid, with gifts
of grace,
Abundant with delicacies
fine,
Welcoming me, honored and free,
With my foes kept at bay right
behind.

Sharing the length of this journey,
Your favor and mercy, my aids,
Each day I abide within Your grace,
Your presence, my life's serenade.

Taking Reflections with You

Think about your past relationship with this great psalm. Has it been a comfort, a "go-to" for you? Why?

Then think about what is opening up.

- How have specific *words and images* in this psalm opened up new meaning for the story of your life?
- How did you sense God's constant companionship in the journey that helped you see God in a new way?
- Did this psalm make you aware of your contentment and discontent? What parts of your life are revealed in a fresh light that gives insight into *who you are*?
- How did your pilgrimage through this short psalm help you reframe your understanding of your *relationship with* God? What would it look like to dwell every day in his presence and eat at His Table?
- What words does Jesus *speak to you* as you sit next to him at the table?
- What do you want to say to him, now that you are sitting with him in this safe place? Go ahead and say it.

Final Embrace

This is a wandering journey that is marked by companionship, not the destination. Read the words as a stroll through an alpine meadow. Feel the sense of being present to a fellow journeyer who is loving being with you. Savor the moments as though they embed you in the day you have been waiting for to find undiminished peace. Let me add that companion comes from com (with) and pan (bread). A companion is one with whom you share bread or a meal. Think about being a Christ-companion as you wander.

Satisfied.
You by my side.
In the countryside.

Me by Your side.
Never denied.
Resting.

Blessing.
Guided, not guessing.
Restoration.
Vivification.
Transformation.
Reframe.
You know my name.
Finally sane.
In Your lane.
Life regained.
Your reputation retained.
Faithful.
Facing death.
Shadow's growing breadth.
Losing life's breath.
Your hand.
My hope.

Protection.
Correction.
Constant connection.
Finding Your location.
Table's affirmation.
Foe's observation.
Host's preparation.
Joining celebration.
Journey's destination.
Abide in Your location.
Hospitality without exception.
Dwell.
Excel.
Companion.
Embraced.
Forever.

Psalm 24

Through the Welcoming Gate to the Place of Belonging

Lift up your heads, you gates; lift them up,
you ancient doors,
that the King of glory may come in.
(Psalm 24:9 NIV)

Surveying the Garden

To whom do you belong?

This psalm is filled with the poetry of belonging with God in his garden.

To whom does this world belong? Who knows they belong to God? Who belongs in God's places of intimate connection? We are drawing closer to finding our lasting home in God's welcoming presence.

We stand before ancient gates. These portals provide access to walled spaces. The gates are about entrance, not exclusion.

Some walls keep people out. Some mark off sacred places. But the gateways before us are to lead us home. We go in, not by our worthiness, but invited by the King of compassion and his Spirit, who says, "Come."

Some people think Jesus has left this world, that his ascension was his exit from earth. But this psalm invites us to see him as the King who, in his ascending, occupying the oval office of heaven. He is always on call, present with us by his Spirit.

In his act of ascension, Jesus extends his reign to all the earth, which belongs to him and to him alone. Jesus is the King of heaven and earth—at the same time.

We stand at the gates of the garden today and walk with him, but our end goal is to enjoy the pleasure of his companionship.

This entrance psalm is a prayer that invites us to soak in God's presence. We are not on a solitary journey. We are sharing this journey with generations of explorers who desired to live within his revealed faithfulness and blessing, finding themselves willing to receive love. Consequently, they overflow with his love in service to God and others.

Feel the Father's royal, glorious arms wrap around you. Hear your soul say, "Abba, I belong to you. Jesus, I belong to you. Spirit, I belong to you."

Into the Garden with God

We left the Shepherd in Psalm 23, but we find ourselves carried by the same Shepherd into terrain where he tends his creation as the glorious King. He never stops being a shepherd. He is the Shepherd King.

This part of the garden is rich with provisions to sustain our mortal bodies, and capabilities to wash our souls. We are more than home. We are in the place of ultimate embrace.

We are with the King who calls us his own. This brings hope. Peter, the disciple who was told to feed Jesus's sheep, told us,

> **And when the Chief Shepherd appears, you will receive the unfading crown of glory.**
> (1 Peter 5:4 NASB)

This is that day!

Do not expect to get your crown in distinction from Jesus. We are given to share his crown, as we abide in him who is our Head in more ways than one. You are a child of the King.

We participate in his life; we do not develop separately. The whole New Testament is a call to live within his life, to depend on his faithful love as fuel for our own.

Passing through the gates, you sense an expansion of your being. You realize that Jesus is not just the king of this place. This is the place from which he cares for the whole world and the universe.

At this moment, you are awakened to the fact that the King of Glory is the bridge between earth and eternity. The word *glory* expands to mean all of the ways the God of heaven expresses himself in the world—glory is his character shining out into the world and to your face. He comes in his Word, his beauty, and his many acts of creating and accompanying all he has made. He speaks to you.

If ever gates could speak, it is these. They say, "Welcome, child." They can speak only because they have been made to cry out by the King who shines his love through them. You do not hear audible words from him, but his Spirit whispers inside you, "We are home." In this moment, you get it—Eternity embraces your humanity—always.

Visions of Paradise

The Welcoming Gate is the invitation to participate in closeness with the Artist who made the world and to whom all things belong. He wants all people, especially you, to go in with him.

Along the Garden Path

As we have noted, other wanderers have walked here before in search of a welcoming space.

Stories and songs can lead us to ancient, ever-new spaces. They point us to the One who made it all. Music clarifies the reality of the artisan, and we are made to enjoy it. The challenge is taking time to listen.

Our vision needs to expand to see that the whole world is holy, made for God to dwell with his people. Our hearing needs to improve to hear his heart.

There is a Welcoming Gate here to celebrate the great realignment between God and humanity. It is set here as a pledge to bring order, based on love, moving out of the chaos of human attempts at control.

The Welcoming Gate is like a trellis. It supports wild and dynamic growth within a structured framework. To blossom fully, beauty needs security and space to develop. That includes a place for you to become more you as one beloved.

The Master Gardener is our guide, but he has a holistic view of our uniqueness. In the garden, there is no competition for attention, only appreciation for the developing whole. Neither do we pursue perfection. When you grow here, it is not an isolated process moving toward maturity. Instead, we flourish in a community with a massive variety and diversity. We are interconnected. We find fulfillment in conformity with Jesus's fearless love, developing clean hands and a pure heart.

A clean heart is *oriented* outward, even though it is *experienced* inwardly. Conscience is a way of inwardly knowing "with God" what is right and wrong, and acting outwardly in the contexts in which we flourish.

When we have a clear conscience, we think in a manner aligned with Jesus. When we depart from that loving harmony, we look away and lose our integrity. We have become hypocrites.

Help comes from spending time with the King of Glory. We need to stop hiding, like Adam and Eve after they became alienated. The ultimate goal in this welcoming journey is to foster a deep face-to-face with God that will bring an overflowing joy.

And so here we are at the gate. We have many walls that stop us, but the one way into the heart of God is to be carried in by Jesus, the King of Glory. All may come in *through* him.

Who is this One who opens ancient portals and unveils the glory of God? It is Jesus; he is the One who has planted his Cross in the field of the world. He has entered the everlasting doors for us so we may know the pleasure of belonging to the God who made us and enjoy his presence daily.

You are at a place where you are already included in a love that will never let you go. Enter with astonishment.

Indwelling the Garden

1 The earth is the LORD's, and all it
contains,
The world, and those who live in it.

The grandeur of this giant globe.
It all belongs to You!
The mountains capped and meadows
robed,
Exist because You choose.

2 For He has founded it upon the seas
And established it upon the rivers.

Seas rise from deep-hid floors,
Coastlands, You patiently hold,
Flowing waters, You adored,
The whole horizon, You did mold.

3 Who may ascend onto the hill of the
LORD?
And who may stand in His holy place?

What grace is granted to climb Your
mount,
To approach Your regal seat?
Who may perch in the intimate still,
In Your mercy-filled retreat?

4 One who has clean hands and a pure
heart,
Who has not lifted up his soul to
deceit
And has not sworn deceitfully.

One whose deeds are moved by love,
Whose heart is always true,
With words that spill out from those
lips
With integrity imbued.

5 He will receive a blessing from
the LORD
And righteousness from the God of
his salvation.

Shower now, Your blessed calm,
As Your nearness lifts my head.
You make me whole, gifted full,
By Your just ways I am led.

6 This is the generation of those who
seek Him,
Who seek Your face—*even* Jacob.
[Selah]

All you seekers, come and find,
Him who is already there,
Join, in joy, with Jacob's heirs,
Eye to eye, within His care.
[I rest in You—I rise to meet you]

7 Lift up your heads, you gates,
And be lifted up, you ancient doors,
That the King of glory may come in!

Raise your eyes, and open wide,
For the entrance of the King.
Clear the way for Him today,
Let the ancient portals swing.

8 Who is the King of glory?
The LORD strong and mighty,
the LORD mighty in battle.

This King of Brilliance, who
is He?
He is the Creator come!
He who fights love's battles;
Our Victory, already won.

9 Lift up your heads, you gates,
And lift *them* up, you ancient doors,
That the King of glory may come in!

Open wide, your ancient ways,
Greet the Dazzling King!
Make His entrance glorious,
Let hosannas ring!

10 Who is this King of glory?
The LORD of armies,
He is the King of glory.
[Selah]

Who is this King of Brilliance?
The Servant King of all,
Always the Astounding One,
Who shines past every wall.
[I rest in You]

Taking Reflections with You

Welcome!

- What words in this psalm attune you to the "place where you belong"?
- How did God's grandeur, as the One to whom the whole earth belongs, allow you to see God in a new way? What comes to mind when you hear Jesus called the King of Glory?
- How did this psalm awaken you to your *sense of yourself*, wanting self-protection, self-affirmation, and feeling worthiness or unworthiness to enter with the King of Glory?
- Did you feel ready to go through the ancient gates and deepen your *relationship with* God? What gets in your way?
- What are the words the King of Glory has to *say to you*? Does his glory diminish you or make you come more fully alive?
- What response, in the *form of words*, do you have as you walk through the Welcoming Gate to belong within its shelter?

Final Embrace

Gates can be placed to keep people or animals out or to make a way to enter. Read as one who has received an invitation and is looking for the entry point. The quest inside is bigger and full of curiosity as each question becomes a gateway to discovery. Listen to each word that resonates with you and let an answer emerge, then release it. Exiting the poem might leave a bit of a tingle in your brain as unexplored openings remain intriguing.

Original ordering.
Universe exploring.
Chaos reordering.
Foundations of Security.

Mountains.
Hills.
Valleys.
Fixed and liquid.

Oceans.
Lakes.
Rivers.
All things flowing and fluid.
All Fields of Flexibility.
Inviting me.
Creation's liturgy.
Marching to eternity.
What will pilgrims see?
Do we have integrity?
What's inside you?
What's inside me?
Do we hide from reality?
Do we live deceitfully?
Is love our actuality?
Can we live honestly?
Can I let the King deliver me?
Let blessings flow?
Dance so all know?
Let all that holds me go.
Let Your grace bestow.
With Your people from long ago.
To Your gates.
Where You wait.
Your arms my final fate.
Never too late.
To enter this gate.
Your glory permeates.
Feeling Your beauty's weight.
Entering Your grand estate.
Living portal.
Unworthy mortal.
Enter.
Now.
Held.
By Glory.
Belonging.

Psalm 25

A Workout in the Way of Wisdom

Show me your ways, Lord, *teach me your paths.*
(Psalm 25:4 NIV)

Surveying the Garden

Fit or fat?

The health of our body and spiritual life both require exercise.

This psalm is structured like a fitness trail, one of those paths with exercise stations along the way for a go-at-your-own-pace workout routine.

Psalm 25 is an acrostic poem, meaning that each verse begins with the following letter of the Hebrew alphabet in consecutive order. It produces a structure for completing the workout in an easily remembered sequence.

The calisthenics (*kallos*—beauty, *sthenos*—strength, ability) exercises we discover in each verse help us shed what is not helpful and build steadfastness in our relationship with the Living God.

Today, we follow a path intended to repeatedly reframe our lives. We are constantly reminded to stop focusing on ourselves and learn to be attentive to the God who already loves us freely.

Psalm 25 takes on a form of liturgy (from *leitourgia*, *laós*—people, *ergon*—work = work of the people, see Philippians 3:3). But its "work" merely enables us to participate in the life of God and not be self-absorbed—it is not about us in the first instance.

Liturgy is not about what "I do" or how we perform specific actions together. It is about facilitating rapt attention, adoration, and being drawn into a faithful relationship with the One who transforms us as we listen, learn, and live together.

Think about getting your body involved in this process. It is so easy to think we are just thinkers. However, this psalm invites us to engage our entire being, including our physical life.

Jesus is putting on his running shoes. Spiritually, we tend to spend time avoiding dealing with our bodies by focusing on our minds. But Jesus is the proof that God values our bodies *and all the rest!* He takes on a human body to be with us. He wants all of us.

With a smile, he nudges you and says, "Let's get you dancing. A cloud of anxiety weighs you down. How about enjoying the beauty of movement for which I made you mine? Let's jazz up your life to follow the moves of the Spirit. The Father gave you his heart; let's get your heart rate healthy enough to tune into his. This may be new to you. It takes time, but it is empowering. Let's get all of you moving!"

Into the Garden with God

Entering the garden with God, we find that Jesus has been transforming our bodies and minds as we get to know him. When we are with him, we feel a love and acceptance that gives us the courage to love others.

Focusing on ourselves creates a fear of others' opinions. This fear pushes us to live in the shadows, immobilizing us with defensiveness. The fear of "what will they say" develops into shame as we imagine the worst.

Hope is the vaccine for fear that aligns us with God's promises for a loving future. We look forward, rather than dwelling on our past failures in the rearview mirror. This is the path to renewal.

Just as vitamins bring out our bodies' vitality, God's love brings out our souls' vitality. The Spirit revitalizes us in knowing and being known by the Living God. The result is shared love, steadfastness, and fitness for the journey.

Once we are free from the judgment of others and confident in the love and faithfulness of Jesus, we are ready to walk, or jog, on with hope. And, as Paul says:

> **And hope does not disappoint, because the love of God has been poured out within our hearts through the Holy Spirit who was given to us.**
> (Romans 5:5 NASB)

This psalm is a workout for learning how to connect with others, not self-improvement.

This passage is not necessarily a religious exercise session. We are learning to be part of a family that works out life together, learning to be creative and loving in the process. Paul ran with Jesus; ultimately, he felt the pleasure of sharing the journey, not looking good or being self-satisfied.

It is time to stretch out and do some exercise. Start by hearing Jesus say, "I love you!" Hear the Father say, "You are My adorable child; you belong to Me!" Hear the Spirit say, "Let's go give gifts to those in need of encouragement, support, counsel, and affirmation. Let's see what love in action can look like today!" Okay, that is a good start. Keep warming up . . .

Visions of Paradise

Now that you are stretched out, let's do some fitness work.

Along the Garden Path

This psalm's path begins with a lifting exercise. I will provide some ideas for other verses to help you think up bodily involvement for yourself, but let's start with an example.

In the first verse, "I put my trust" is how the NIV translates the first Hebrew word, *nephesh*. I prefer the translation, "I lift up." That rendition points to an exercise of lifting. What is "lifted" is embodied in the Hebrew word *nephesh*, the second word in the verse. The word *soul* is often used in the NIV to translate this idea. A more vibrant and complete image would recognize *nephesh* as *our whole living being*. We are lifting all of ourselves up to the Lord.

Let's translate this "lifting all of our living selves" into action.

Start by reaching down to your toes. Sweep your hands past your whole body. Your legs symbolize your movements, your stomach speaks of appetites, your heart refers to your emotions, and your head implies your thinking. In brief, sweep your hands from your toes past to above your head. Hand everything you have gathered from your self-awareness over to the embrace of the Father. He is there waiting. Repeat until you have given yourself over to freeing yourself to trust your true Father.

Engaging your body with your thinking and feeling is a whole-life workout.

The world today works in a process of dehumanization. In it, you are an object, a worker bee, a cog, in the modern mechanistic world—you are part of the machine. We are revitalizing who you are as God's person.

Entering this psalm is a process intended to rehumanize you. You are not a thing; you are a person. And you need to be nurtured to grow in your personal relationships. Release yourself into the love of this personal God. He has already reached out to you.

Here is a list of spiritual exercises that capture the essence of each verse, corresponding to physical exercises. Pray and discover hand and body motions that might express these spiritual ideas. It is even better if you share them with someone:

Verse 2 – *Shame drop—What do you hide about yourself?*

Verse 3 – *Entwining our heart with God's—What in you reaches out for more of God's heart?*

Verse 4 – *Balancing walk—What are your priorities and how do you balance them with God's?*

Verse 5 – *Reaching out for support—Who do you need to let love you?*

Verse 6 – *Remembering who supports us—In whom are you being grounded?*

Verse 7 – *Pressing through forgetting and remembering—What needs letting go? What needs celebrating?*

Verse 8 – *Rhythms of walking back and forward—What could you mend and dream about?*

Verse 9 – *Humble walk on a straight line—In what areas do you think too much or too little of yourself?*

Verse 10 – *Bowing in honor of God's presence—Where could you bow and acknowledge God's gifts and company?*

Verse 11 – *Washing away my past—What pollutes your thoughts that need serious washing?*

Verse 12 – *Head and neck stretch to learn to choose direction—Where is creativity lacking?*

Verse 13 – *Passing hope to future generations—Who are you stretching to dream for?*

Verse 14 – *The movements of friendship with God and others—What could be an act of friendship for you today?*

Verse 15 – *Panoramic searching to see God all around—Do a memory and future scan; do you see what God is doing?*

Verse 16 – *Embracing partners, present and distant—Are you communicating how you value those who are your life partners?*

Verse 17 – *Washing worries from your mind—What do you need to give up about tomorrow?*

Verse 18 – *Lunging into forgiveness—Who do you need to stop judging even as you remember the pain they caused?*

Verse 19 – *Running from enemies—Who do you need to let go of, as not part of your tribe, as an act of liberation?*

Verse 20 – *Stance held by one defended by another—Who do you need God to be your refuge from, to keep you secure?*

Verse 21 – *Jumping jacks of obedient trust—How do you let your body tell you all will be well?*

Verse 22 – *Arm circles reaching out to the community—Who do you need to reach out to as pilgrims on your journey?*

Each of these exercises is an example of attentiveness and involvement. They are mental, spiritual, and physical aspects.

The goal is to relieve stress and anxiety, and to become attentive to specific validation for your life that can only come from God. You are exercising relational muscles.

This whole psalm envisions walking a path called the Torah. We are exploring a way of walking, exercising our whole being in correspondence with God.

The path ahead transforms our delights and shapes us to endure suffering. We are prepared to be resilient in the simplicity and complexity of navigating life with God. There may be a conviction of past failure—that must be released. There will be instructions for reframing our future within God's presence, which must be embraced.

You are ready and warmed up to enter. Feel the rhythms of renewal.

Indwelling the Garden

1 To You, LORD, I lift up my soul.
2 My God, in You I trust,
Do not let me be ashamed;
Do not let my enemies rejoice
over me.

3 Indeed, none of those who wait for
You will be ashamed;
Those who deal treacherously
without cause will be ashamed.
4 Make me know Your ways, LORD;
Teach me Your paths.

5 Lead me in Your truth and teach me,
For You are the God of my salvation;
For You I wait all the day.
6 Remember, LORD, Your compassion
and Your faithfulness,
For they have been from of old.

Enhance my endeavors,
Give my wings feathers,
I release my cares to You.
Protect me from harms,
From crushing alarms,
Surrounded by Your safety true.

With confidence clear,
Overcome shame or fear,
Unlike those who stand alone.
Open the way,
To be near You this day;
Make Your delight wisely known.

Give me a keen ear,
That Your way I may steer,
Listening for You, Heart of hearts.
Recall promises made,
Your refrain long replayed,
Compassion and love You impart.

[7]Do not remember the sins of my
youth or my wrongdoings;
Remember me according to Your
faithfulness,
For Your goodness' sake, LORD.
[8]The LORD is good and upright;
Therefore He instructs sinners in the
way.
[9]He leads the humble in justice,
And He teaches the humble His way.
[10]All the paths of the LORD are
faithfulness and truth
To those who comply with His
covenant and His testimonies.

[11]For the sake of Your name, LORD,
Forgive my wrongdoing, for it is
great.
[12]Who is the person who fears the
LORD?
He will instruct him in the way he
should choose.

[13]His soul will dwell in prosperity,
And his descendants will inherit the
land.
[14]The secret of the LORD is for those
who fear Him,
And He will make them know His
covenant.

[15]My eyes are continually toward
the LORD,
For He will rescue my feet from the
net.
[16]Turn to me and be gracious to me,
For I am lonely and afflicted.

Forgive my folly,
Your kindness, my finale,
May Your goodness over me lay.
Be my true Guide,
Help the fearful who hide,
Only You can lead us Your way.

Your course is set sure
And the lowly You cure,
Calling to walk by Your side.
Each step that You take,
With compassion You make,
To bless all those who abide.

Released from guilt's burden,
You save me from ruin,
My storm is calmed by Your voice.
You search eye to eye
Love's modus operandi
Leading, to follow Your choice.

This inheritance of blessing,
Is the heart's one true wellspring,
My kin shall abound on this land.
Your intimate counsel
Fills the humble one's mainsail
Led by Your covenanting hand.

Intent now to follow,
Exhumed from the hollow,
Only You can free me to stand.
While in this saddened silence,
Meet my fears with confidence,
Hold me, so my life may expand.

[17] The troubles of my heart are
enlarged;
Bring me out of my distresses.
[18] Look at my misery and my trouble,
And forgive all my sins.

[19] Look at my enemies, for they are
many,
And they hate me with violent
hatred.
[20] Guard my soul and save me;
Do not let me be ashamed, for I take
refuge in You.

[21] Let integrity and uprightness
protect me,
For I wait for You.
[22] Redeem Israel, God,
From all his distress.

Drain all my tension,
Restore my attention,
Rescue me now to Your place.
Pour salve on all my sorrows,
Acquit my tomorrows,
Refreshed by Your healing face.
Stave the pressing onslaught
That infests my heart with
hate-rot,
Until my energy is gone.
Escort, as I walk,
My one sturdy Rock,
Shelter me, calm in Your dawn.

Can You see that I'm waiting,
By Your power operating,
Content to sit here with You
still?
Your heart brings us back
From our place of lack,
To finally rejoice in Your will.

Taking Reflections with You

- What words in this psalm gave you a "workout" that you have not had before? Were you stretched to see new parts of "the whole of you" that needed attention?
- How did God's covenant promises help you to endure the workout? Could you see the already active God who coaches and contains your life? Could you feel him nurturing you to fitness, seeing God in a new, supportive way?
- Did this psalm help you to feel how important your body is in being a healthy person? Could you see that calisthenics are forms of attentiveness helping shape *who you are*?
- What did sharing the process of becoming fit as a person look like in your *relationship with God*? Is it just about you, or

is God already at work as far as you can tell? What is a "fit" relationship with God in your understanding?

- Could you hear the voice of Jesus in this workout? What words did you hear that encouraged you?
- What words capture how you feel at the end of the challenge course that articulate how you feel and want to respond to God? They may be gratitude, exhaustion, or dawning awareness that needs to be explored.

Final Embrace

Transformation takes time. The intent to foster healthy growth motivates acts to explore what is possible. We cannot see the end, but we can see the next step. What follows is a final victory lap to affirm that the journey is worthwhile.

Trimming trail of trials.
Sweating miles.
Searching for Your smile.
Shedding the shaming.
Guilt reframing.
Lifting.
Raising.
Praising.
Hoping in waiting.
From the dust.
Now to trust.
On this journey.
Not in a hurry.
Faithful.
Available.
Teachable.
Follow Your way.
Aligned to stay.
Constant to pray.
Mindful.
Heartful.
Faithful still.
Up this hill.
Borne by your will.
You will always be.
Patient.
Kind.
Merciful.
Loving.
Forgiving.
Be that.
For me.
Forget my failing.
All my flailing.
Youthful derailing.
Humbling.
Tumbling.
Forward.
Down Your path.
Do the math.
It all adds up to You.
I'm learning awe.
From all I saw.
I drop my jaw.

You want to be friends.
You look.
You see.
You rescue me.
From every snare.
Always there.
Compassion rare.
Rinse away despair.
Sheltering repair.
Enveloped in Your care.
Preserved.
In community.
On my knee.
With family.
Victorious.
Shared Celebratory.

Psalm 26

Walkabout to the Mercy Seat

Test me, Lord, *and try me, examine my heart and my mind.*
(Psalm 26:2 NIV)

Surveying the Garden

Judging eyes.

Do you ever feel the accusing glances of others?

When others scrutinize us critically, we plead for innocence. How can others know what is happening in our situations? We get defensive. We sense our own integrity and want support.

In the face of God's presence, we plead for mercy. We know we are imperfect. He knows us supremely, with all our weaknesses and inadequacies. Yet, he loves us and faithfully restores us through his grace.

In God's mercy, he sees our deficiencies and seeks to restore us to wholeness. Mercy is his medicinal mending for what distresses us. We yearn to come home to a continual embrace with this reliable God, even though we cannot imagine that state in all our obliviousness.

We are heading toward the mercy seat, once housed in the tent of meeting in the wilderness.

We are going to see the Judge. Does your mind jump to fearful condemnation?

The Living God diagnoses what ails us, brings cleansing that settles our souls, and refines us through his faithfulness. Trust translates into tranquility.

Imagine Jesus is coming to meet you, accompanied by two cherubim. These angelic figures were placed face-to-face on top of the Ark of the covenant in the Holy of Holies. With covering wings, they are promises of God's faithful love, reminders that God makes a way to be judged and made whole by his holy love.

Jesus and his sentries walk with you. They start to sing. You feel spiritually refreshed as the splashes of mercy shower you with a warming, cleansing bath.

All accusative voices start to fade. You are beginning to feel clean and connected.

Jesus says, "Sit with me now on the mercy seat. This sitting place is not for you alone; it is a meeting place. Sit with My promises. Sense my covering. Let My mercy bring you home to Me. Be with Me; let the rest drift away."

Into the Garden with God

It is easy to think that God is watching and especially judging. Hiding is an intuitive response.

We question whether we are living up to his expectations. Avoidance is easier than acknowledgment.

In actuality, all that noise in our heads is not his fault-finding inquisition. It is our fear of failure. Or worse yet, the voice of the Accuser, who focuses on what is missing, centering us on supposed inadequacies.

Jesus is the savior of our souls. Some think that means he is a life insurance policy to keep us from hell. It is more accurate to see salvation as God's diagnosis of what destroys us and his activity to restore us.

The Living God moves us toward wholeness in our relationships, encompassing our thoughts, emotions, behaviors, and all that flows from them.

In our alienation from God and others, we calcify into people with hard hearts, becoming unavailable for love.

All our judgments flow from our fear. We are inclined to defend ourselves and diminish others' judgments and values, all in an attempt to feel secure.

But Jesus says,

> "Do not judge, so that you will not be judged. [2] For in the way you judge, you will be judged; and by your standard of measure, it will be measured to you."
> (Matthew 7:1–2 NASB)

Jesus wants us to stop judging ourselves and others. Paul continues this theme, saying,

> **I care very little if I am judged by you or by any human court; indeed, I do not even judge myself.**
> (1 Corinthians 4:3 NIV)

We must recognize that our judgments are always incomplete; however, we may not be aware of this. Jesus and Paul want us to throw judgment out with the trash—except to ask what love compels us to do.

When you are in God's garden, stop evaluating yourself. He wants to roll away the stones in your heart, and mercy has that power.

Let your complaints (the standard form of judging) go. As leaves cling to the branch for the winter, yet are released with spring's fresh sap, let mercy deliver others and yourself from fear's constraints that you might be doing it wrong.

Jesus says: "Drop all those heavy judgments. Come, soak in the mercy that flows from the grace of My self-giving. Let it penetrate your callouses. I see where they have developed in your heart, mind, and body. They have muted your sensitivity to the touch of love. Let mercy flow so you may feel alive again."

Visions of Paradise

The mercy seat is a place to get cleaned out on the inside. We all need it, but we are all ignorant of how much!

Along the Garden Path

You are walking this path with the Judge who has been judged in your place. Let him judge, release your fear, and free you to rest in his mercy.

Consider the degree to which you have made yourself the judge of what will sustain you. Self-protection develops into self-trusting, leaving us with a biased perspective, looking out for ourselves.

This psalm prompts us to learn the difference between arrogance and confidence. One is about ourselves, and the other is about our relationship to others.

The goal of the psalm is peace with God as a faithful companion, clean and released.

The mercy seat brings us to God's kind of peace, releasing us from whatever deflates our spiritual life.

Hand over all attempts to clear your conscience. Leave room for the Holy Spirit, the breath of God, to fill you up with song and dance. Invite the gaze of God's light to remove the worry and fill you with humility and integrity.

Let Jesus examine your heart and mind. Let him probe every thought. He will make room for a new conscience attuned to his love.

Make the walk of your life one of shedding the wounds and finding wonder. That is the walkabout of worship. It will keep bringing you back to the mercy seat. Jesus will always prepare you for the next chapter if you stay on his walkabout.

He offers a bowl to wash your hands, readying you for the coming meal. He invites you to his table, an altar not for sacrifice but for a family meal. It is full of remembrance of his compassion and grace. It prepares us for the mercy seat and then celebrates its impact.

See how his glory shines in his habitation, where the mercy flows as splendor and light brushes over you. His beauty is the form of holiness that dazzles, surrounds, and penetrates you with attentive love.

You are in the house of the Father's love. It is not fixed in one place; it is the temple of his presence where Jesus and the Spirit mediate his companionship. His heart looms large and envelops you with pristine peace. Let him permeate your brittle or tough places.

God's glory is not vague brightness but is the intensity of God's lovingkindness, which becomes personally transformative, opening you like a flower in the warmth of spring's awakening sun.

God's mercy seat is shared with you. Jesus rises to welcome you to sit and begin his most loving examination. He scans your soul and heals with profound mercy to restore your wholeness. There is nothing you can do but accept what only he can give.

Indwelling the Garden

[1] Vindicate me, LORD, for I have walked in my integrity,
And I have trusted in the LORD without wavering.

Support me in the court of life
Defend my faithful ways,
You know I cling to Your every word,
Attentive all my days.

[2] Examine me, LORD, and put me to the test;
Refine my mind and my heart.

See if I'm pure, with Your scrutiny sure
To find any failing faults,
Consider my thoughts and what I hold dear
Content that in You I exalt.

[3] For Your goodness is before my eyes,
And I have walked in Your truth.

I open my eyes to gaze at You,
In awe of dependable love.
I echo Your gaze, learn faithful ways,
Transformed by Your love from above.

[4] I do not sit with deceitful people,
Nor will I go with pretenders.

I steer away from worthless walks,
Where empty stories flow.
If sitting there, I'm fully aware
That my honesty is low.

[5] I hate the assembly of evildoers,
And I will not sit with the wicked.

When frustrated by that fractured fray,
A gathered hall of lies,
My soul drains low, devoid of peace,
My body turns to fly.

6 I will wash my hands in innocence,
And I will go around Your altar,
LORD,

Cleanse me from the inside out,
A clean and willing soul,
Feed me at Your table, endeared,
That I may be made whole.

7 That I may proclaim with the voice
of thanksgiving
And declare all Your wonders.

I fill each day with thanksgiving,
Grateful for all You have done,
At sunrise I celebrate Your stunning
feats,
The victories You have won.

8 LORD, I love the dwelling of Your
house,
And the place where Your glory
remains.

I love to be at home with You,
To feel your presence full.
Your delight dances within these
walls.
I'm transformed by Your Spirit's
pull.

9 Do not take my soul away *along* with
sinners,
Nor my life with men of bloodshed,

Never let me drift away,
Drawn by a devious foil.
Keep me from those flocks of fools,
Departing with other's spoil.

10 In whose hands is a wicked scheme,
And whose right hand is full of
bribes.

Protect me from their sleight of hand,
They never show what's true,
Shield from weasels, intent to steal,
Whose dealings are corruptly
shrewd.

11 But as for me, I will walk in my
integrity;
Redeem me, and be gracious to me.

With head held high and a humble
heart,
I spend my days by Your side,
Fiascos wither in the wind,
As mercy covers me, and in You I
abide.

12 My foot stands on level ground;
In the congregations I will bless
the LORD.

Bathed in the splendor of an anthem
sung,
With my conscience cleaned to joy,
I celebrate this risen morn,
With love's gusto wholly deployed.

Taking Reflections with You

- What *words* in this psalm touched on deep issues of judgment? What accusers or critical voices do you need to have washed from your life?
- How did God's offering of mercy wash over you? How did his restoration open your eyes to see God's reviving at work?
- How did this psalm open your ears to hear tension in your internal life? How did that awareness help you see more of *who you are*?
- What do your emotions about judging and being judged say about your *relationship with God*? Do you experience God, other humans, or your inner demons as your chief critics?
- What does it look like to shed all accusations of inadequacy and *hear new words from God* that speak his words of mercy?
- What words can you hear flow *from your mouth or heart* when mercy has washed you clean for this new day?

Final Embrace

The mercy seat is not your everyday furniture. It is a place to sit where you know that God's mercy never leaves you. As you read the words, let them wash over you with mercy, meaning to remove all the judgment, complaints, rebuffing, and rejection to feel restored, inside and out, and ready to be clean in your conscience as one set free.

Innocence.
Faithful persistence.
Judgment resistance.
Looking for resilience.
Never balking.
No slipping or sliding.
Avoiding hiding.
Go where You're guiding.
No doubting.
Not pouting.
Rightly rerouting.
Integrity igniting.
Test me.
Try me.
Look right inside me.
Burn pure.
I can endure.
Your heart I prefer.

Your love, my cure.
Your truth I procure.
Kindness.
Beyond the blindness.
Get that behind us.
Align me with Your justice.
Unhinged from the faithless.
Your aspirations ahead of us.
Hands.
Washed.
Clean.
Heart.
Redeemed.
At Your table.
Esteemed.
Your glory beams.
Circling and singing.
Harmony's glory ringing.
Your presence bedazzling.
Your wonders resounding.
We are here to harmonize.
Looking eyes to eyes.
Nothing to analyze.
This is the prize.
Earthy.
Unworthy.
Some days are quirky.
Others perky.
Forever bathed.
In.
Your.
Mercy.

Psalm 27

To Gaze on the Light of Beauty

My heart says of you, "Seek his face!"
Your face, LORD, I will seek.
(Psalm 27:8 NIV)

Surveying the Garden

Fear breeds in the darkness. Fear is dispelled by light.

Today, we enter a place filled with God's light, radiating from God's face to disperse fear.

Fear lurks in shadowed remembrances, prowling in the backstory of our losses, disappointments, and confrontations.

These buried encounters fill the library of our memories with things we would like to forget. However, they spill out from the shelves of our minds as mementos, setting off emotional alarms when things start looking bad.

We are usually unaware of our fears until they are surging through us. Yet they are there, riskily waiting in hiding.

It is worth becoming aware of our fears to move beyond them. Let's try a mental exercise to gain access.

- I occasionally encourage two people to look at each other and say, "I am not afraid of you." This is generally easy and even brings a chuckle.

- Then, I ask them to tell each other *what they think of the other*. This is a challenge for most because we secretly fear what the other will think of our feelings about them.
- Next, I request that each tell the other *what they think of themselves*. Further resistance ensues. Why? Because self-revelation does not feel safe. We may betray our arrogance or naive innocence. It feels risky.
- Finally, I ask each person to tell the other *what they think that person thinks of them*. This is most challenging because we do not usually think about or reveal this personal depth. This is where face-to-face authenticity and connection begin. In truth, we relate to others based on what we think others feel about us. If we think they like us, all is well; if not, we resist or hide—we relate to our perception, not the actuality. Our task today is to pursue acceptance without fear of rejection.

Fear will always be the brake pedal in our lives, stopping us. We need to find the gas pedal.

To walk in the light is to be fearlessly seen and loved, and love in reply. All becomes open, and we feel free to be ourselves. This is where friendship approaches the intimacy of the heart. Both persons are released to come out to play and share unafraid. Some never experience this and live with masks and walls of protection for their lifetime.

Honest disclosure opens the possibility of discovering the depth of another's beauty and authentic stature. The greatest wonder and joy occur when this openness is reflected back to you.

Authenticity is the entryway to personal connection in knowing and being known.

Jesus is the revealing light of the world, but he can feel distant and taken for granted. He invites you to walk closely with him and see more deeply than ever your hidden fears and the possibilities beyond those fears.

He says: "Don't trust me because I tell you to. Let me reveal to you who I am, what holds you back, and what reality looks like. Fear is only a smokescreen to cover over reality. Trust Me only if you find me trustworthy. Dive into the mystery with Me and realize My love was already there. Let's go discovering."

Into the Garden with God

When the sun shines, the world is revealed to us. But we often forget it is there. The psalmist beckons us to the beauty of light shining and reflecting in the world.

Reflections are images that connect us with reality that is otherwise unavailable. For example, we cannot see the nose on our face without a mirror. We need a reflection to see what is really there. We cannot see God face-to-face, but we can hear echoes of his voice and see his work in the world.

Paul the Apostle yearned for this face-to-face kind of meeting with Jesus. At the pinnacle of 1 Corinthians, Paul echoes the psalmist's desire to gaze on the beauty of God. Paul endures with dark, reflected images, as when you see someone behind you in the mirror. But he is drawn to the love yet to be fulfilled in a future face-to-face encounter. He trumpets out,

> **For now we see in a mirror dimly, but then face to face; now I know in part, but then I will know fully, just as I also have been fully known.**
> (1 Corinthians 13:12 NASB)

This is the sweet spot of intimacy—knowing and being known.

The gospel's end game is face-to-face intimacy. The complete revelation is yet to come. We are in a time between the times. We remember Jesus's past, enjoy his present accompaniment from heaven, and anticipate his return—we wait and worship with hope and trust.

The Spirit of Jesus and his Father open our ears and eyes to see Jesus. He is reflected in the Bible and the life of the gathered body of Christ. He is here in the room with us. Listen for him.

All the kaleidoscopic images of him in the Bible come together to say, "Here I am!"

Jesus smiles at you and starts to hum. You find yourself starting to hum in response to him. He is awakening in you an old song you love to sing. He walks to the far side of the reflecting pool that has appeared, and you see Jesus's reflection in the still water. Each image results from the interplay of light, body, and interaction with this place and his presence. Humming, you dive in.

Visions of Paradise

Let Jesus clean out the cobwebs of your soul and flood you with his light as you dive into his love.

Along the Garden Path

You are on the path that leads to the delight of being with the Living Lord.

But guess what—he is already with you! You are on the way to his dwelling place, your heart's true home.

Can you feel the weight of your day behind you? Weight is the heaviness that comes with awareness of unfulfilled tasks, complicated interactions, imperfect relationships, and the fear that tomorrow will be more of the same.

How hidden and deep are those oppressors who belittle or dominate you from the past? Their presence gives meaning to the idea of community trauma as a constant threat to you. Their violence may be verbal or physical as they besiege your emotional life. They may be enemies or those who are close and control you. Our prisons are often veiled.

Hope comes with the discovery of the Person who embodies free personhood. That experience is encompassed in the enjoyment of communion with the One who calls you his own.

We need this healing shelter of the One who gives us security within the encircling of his arms.

We need his holiness, which does not mean cleaning up our act. His holiness comes when the troubles of the past find resolution in the resilience of coming home to the Abba of Jesus, arm in arm with Jesus, and guided by the Spirit.

When set free from the reactivity of past traumas, we feel gratitude, an extra bounce in our steps, and we shout relief and praise. Celebration becomes a responsive rush of empowerment, which is the gift of the Spirit.

We come, wanting to be met. Our internal voice prompts us, saying, "Listen to him, look into his eyes, and let his whole face embrace you. Let his heart hold and mold your heart to wholeness again."

Often, however, that old voice of fear creeps in. . . . "He will not have time for you. He has more important people to attend to. If he really looks close, he will see everything you hide inside." You are plagued with an orphan's heart.

You feel abandoned when the loss of love, friendship, and even your parents' affection has left you.

Then his light floods in. Fears flee because they have no reality in the face of his light. The present provision by the One who made you leads you with confidence to find your heart's true treasure.

This treasure hunt becomes a humble quest to find, or to be found, within the creative life born of the Spirit. You blossom because you go with this One who brings out the best in you. Transformation is possible because he ignites a love that refines your intentions and actions.

He realigns your active life to ask, "What is the loving thing to do?" in each situation. That loving thing has only one source—the heart of the Father.

Trustworthy love is not a general style of love born by human design. This dynamic, daily sculpted form of love is the Spirit's kind, constant, and attentive love, which bears his fruit.

You are now in the land of the living. You are a person who is walking with this personal God.

An intense hope surges in you. You feel a strength not your own, but from being with him. He makes you courageous.

Developing trust fosters a true sense of companionship, enabling shared experiences, much like setting off on an adventure with a reliable guide. Your confidence grows as the guide's competence plays out again and again.

Through this attachment, you are astounded by the magnificence of this One you have come to trust, who makes the journey possible and profoundly worthwhile.

The Light of the World invites you to follow him fearlessly as he strides along the way before you to the heart of his Father.

Indwelling the Garden

1 The LORD is my light and my
 salvation;
Whom should I fear?
The LORD is the defense of my life;
Whom should I dread?

Luminescent LORD of all my life.
 What worry shall I hold?
Encompassed by Your steadfast care,
 What darkness can enfold?

2 When evildoers came upon me to
 devour my flesh,
My adversaries and my enemies, they
 stumbled and fell.

Prowling stalkers surround my space,
 Seeking to snatch by surprise,
But they fall away, tripped up in foul
 play,
 While You gently help me rise.

3 If an army encamps against me,
My heart will not fear;
If war arises against me,
In spite of this I am confident.

Though encircled in the night,
 My heart will calmly beat.
Even in the midst of war,
 I will not fear defeat.

4 One thing I have asked from the
LORD, that I shall seek:
That I may dwell in the house of the
LORD all the days of my life,
To behold the beauty of the
LORD
And to meditate in His temple.

One request shall light my path,
My yearning's hope to find,
To reside within Your beauty,
Where delight will fill my mind.

5 For on the day of trouble He will
conceal me in His tabernacle;
He will hide me in the secret place of
His tent;
He will lift me up on a rock.

Every hour, You will hide me,
Safe within Your tent,
With loving stealth, You veil my sight,
Evading hearts ill-bent.

6 And now my head will be lifted up
above my enemies around me,
And I will offer sacrifices in His tent
with shouts of joy;
I will sing, yes, I will sing praises to
the LORD.

Once again my blinking eyes
Shall see the light of day.
I will arise with dancing delight,
And whistle while I play.

7 Hear, LORD, when I cry with my
voice,
And be gracious to me and answer
me.

Listen, oh LORD, to my longing lament,
Lost in the lonely night.
Let Your restoring reassurance reply,
Rest me in Your sight.

8 When *You said*, "Seek My face," my
heart said to You,
"I shall seek Your face, LORD."

While Your whisper wound its way,
Saying, "Look into My eyes,"
I breathed a yearning deep return,
"Your gaze is my only prize."

9 Do not hide Your face from me,
Do not turn Your servant away in anger;
You have been my help;
Do not abandon me nor forsake me,
God of my salvation!

Please play no games, where I must
seek,
To find Your presence hid.
Never leave me all alone,
Let Your comfort calm this kid.

10 For my father and my mother have
forsaken me,
But the LORD will take me up.

I've outgrown the security
Of my childhood home.
I trust now Your encouragement,
From which I will never roam.

[11] Teach me Your way, LORD,
And lead me on a level path
Because of my enemies.

Save me from the ambush,
When the bullies await.
I will follow You in safety,
Never wanting to separate.

[12] Do not turn me over to the desire of my enemies,
For false witnesses have risen against me,
And the violent witness.

My tormentors seek to slur my name,
Gathering accusers all around,
They slander the repute of helpless lives,
Howling like hungry hounds.

[13] I certainly believed that I would see the goodness of the LORD
In the land of the living.

Completely drained, I would have been,
Except You held my hand,
Sustained alone by Your kindly heart,
Displayed throughout the land.

[14] Wait for the LORD;
Be strong and let your heart take courage;
Yes, wait for the LORD.

This I can say, patiently wait,
Set your hope on Him,
Know that He will keep His word,
His light will never dim.

Taking Reflections with You

- What *words in this psalm* reveal emotions from the light of love or the shadows of fear?
- How did you see God's light touch your dark places and the fears of dangerous, threatening, or unsafe people? How did you see God as the source of hope in a new way?
- How did this psalm reveal fear that is present and active in your life? What did your new awareness of fear allow you to see about *who you are*? Are you ever defined by your fears?
- How do your fears direct your *relationship with* God, helping or minimizing your sense of intimacy with God?
- What *words from Jesus* would cast a healing light on your life?
- What *words can you say* to Jesus with no fear?

Final Embrace

Look in a mirror. See how it connects you with the world, not just your image. It points you to reality, rather than disconnecting from it. Sometimes, like with your face, it is your only access. Then look more deeply beyond the seen and listen for the voice that echoes, "I see you to your heart's deepest level. I will hold you there."

Beauty bright.
Exhuming fright.
Hidden fears made right.
Facing trauma.
Dread's panorama.
Life after mama.
Now.
One.
Thing.
With You.
My only view.
Inquiring preview.
Beholding You true.
The One I look to.
Watching You come through.
With my life askew.
Enemies subdued.
Thank you.
Hiding in Your tent.
No matter where I went.
Letting me vent.
Until I am spent.
Renewal time.
Listen to me whine.
Please be kind.
Real answers.
I need to find.

My Heart.
Seeks.
Your face.
Eager for grace.
Eye to eye.
While lost in space.
Parents left me.
Without anybody.
Will You care for me?
Teach me.
Hold me.
Lead me.
Unfold the road before me?
Guard me.
Defend me.
Believe in me.
Goodness.
Here and now.
Walking proud.
To live out loud.
Brave.
Strong.
Stubborn.
Confident.
With You.
Pleased.

Psalm 28

Emergency Prayer

Praise be to the Lord, *for he has heard my cry for mercy.*

(Psalm 28:6 NIV)

Surveying the Garden

"Someone call 911; we need help!"

This pleading request acknowledges a desperate situation that demands immediate attention.

In the game of life, the need for rescue always lurks in the field of possibilities as we face the unknown. All we can do is prepare ourselves for emergencies, confrontations, and tragedies.

One may think gardens are all about tranquility. However, there can be places where insight and assistance are needed on many levels. Disease and intruders are ever present. Lack of care, neglected nurturing, and ignored pruning diminish health in the whole landscape of our lives.

Over our lifespan, we may encounter a life-threatening medical event, unexpected disputes, or persistent conflict. Things get out of control with tragic consequences.

Having exhausted our resources and wisdom, we need to seek help from someone adequate for the situation.

Today, we are visiting a place of connection amidst desperation. This place is significant because it reminds us that we need not live insecurely. We can call for help; this is the place to connect with the right person.

Jesus stands inside the gate, waiting. He can sense your challenged mental and emotional state. He says, "I can see into the deep part of you. If you call, I will answer. Recognizing my presence will always be the start of the answer. Breathe. Close your eyes. Let my presence wash through you from head to toe. Let my embrace relax you."

Into the Garden with God

Living in conflicted times is a constant theme of the Bible. The book of Revelation ends the Bible with many cries for help, containing almost one hundred quotes and allusions from the Psalms. In Psalm 28 and the book of Revelation, we witness the 911 call of the saints addressing heaven. Jesus responds to set all things right.

Jesus does not just care for a few. He is healing for all people.

Jesus meets us in this psalm in a manner similar to when he met the disciples in his time on earth. He comes as the ever-present help and knows what is needed—he is sufficient to the task. He is a first responder and a last responder. In the end, he wraps up his restoration work. It may not be what you expected.

John's vision became the book of Revelation, a revelation of God's final dealing with all that is amiss in the human experience. Psalm 28 takes us to a similar place. What is essential is knowing whom to call.

In the final chapter of the Bible, the human crises persist, but the answer becomes more obvious. Jesus offers help, saying,

> "Behold, I am coming quickly, and My reward *is* with Me, to
> reward each one as his work deserves. [13] I am the Alpha and the
> Omega, the first and the last, the beginning and the end. . . ."
> [17] The Spirit and the bride say, "Come." And let the one who
> hears say, "Come." And let the one who is thirsty come; let the
> one who desires, take the water of life without cost.
> (Revelation 22:12–13, 17 NASB)

Jesus answers the cry of a needy world with embodied grace—himself. The Spirit and the Church are the Grand Invitation to answer his call—Come!

Jesus and the Spirit answer our call for help with an unconditional and overflowing provision to meet the deepest human needs. "Come. Drink. Live. Answer our call!"

Jesus takes you to his phone booth in the garden and says: "I have set up meeting places in the wilderness as a reminder that I am available. You need a place to connect when you are overwhelmed. Come here to this place, this psalm. Cry out. I am always on call. There are no collect calls. This is a listening space to remember I am always available. Let's step inside and feel the anticipation of connection."

Visions of Paradise

The psalm can become a mental space, just like the thought of being in your bed. Here we have a booth for connecting. Step into the booth and sense the presence of possibility. Like prayer, Jesus is always there, though our eyes limit our awareness. Stop and prepare to chat with the One who comes alongside to help.

Along the Garden Path

Next to the entrance of this path, a big rock sits as a reminder. God loves to leave memory aids of his resiliency.

Israel set up piles of rocks in the wilderness to remind them of God's faithfulness. Jesus is the Rock who lives God's faithfulness, who is ancient and set there for us by God to this day.

In all our crises and calls for help, Jesus's presence precedes our pleas for rescue.

We cannot stand the thought that God may turn away when we are desperate. Loneliness and depression seep in with his perceived absence, ending any sense of security in life. It may lead to apathy.

So we need to reach out and get our bodies in action. We may use words or raise our hands, just like kids, to get attention. Our hands focus and direct our whole being so we may enter a position of surrendered prayer.

This is an opening, yielding moment. We intend to share space with him, recognizing that he has already been waiting to meet with us. Our whole body, mind, and words are now focused on hearing and being heard—embraced inside and out.

We wish the humans around us had more compassion. You probably know who they are for you. It is so hard to continue with such callous and obnoxious bystanders in our lives. Unintentionally, our concern for ourselves quickly becomes a wall against them, and the world divides and disintegrates. Awareness of others' disregard does not mean they are not intrusive in our emotions.

So, while we lift our hands to heaven for help, we fear others may pickpocket us. People seem to want something *from* us more than *for* us. They fail to value us, creating a grinding dissonance. Their inattentive ways become distant as they develop priorities that are not important to us.

In the quagmire of our complex lives, prayers turn from a pursuit of God to angst about our future. Hopes are breathed as half prayer, half complaint—until we remember to give thanks. We remember to "thank it forward," focusing on blessings yet to come.

Jesus is the Great Mediator between all relationships that fall apart. When we concentrate on him, we know we have been heard, and he will lead us.

Having been heard, our hearts are calmed from anxiety and kick-started to rejoice. Our ears hear new music, smooth as honey, sweeping us into a delightful dance. This turn of attention is not self-generated. It is authentic worship energized by trust in the One who gives strength.

The Holy Spirit, which flows from this Anointed One, aligns a whole crowd of people. His family surrounds you in one movement of dynamic response, following the One who is sometimes king, sometimes shepherd, and in this moment is the responder to the 911 call. The crisis is over. The celebration has begun. You are not alone.

You are being borne on eagle's wings once again. The Great Shepherd is holding you. You feel the security of those arms. The menagerie of mangled memories is whisked away. You are held.

Stay embraced as you enter the psalm.

Indwelling the Garden

1 To You, LORD, I call;
My rock, do not be deaf to me,
For if You are silent to me,
I will become like those who go down
to the pit.

Resounds again, my anguished need,
I shatter in the hush.
Firm Forever, extend Your ear,
In this chasm, I'm being crushed.

2 Hear the sound of my pleadings
when I cry to You for help,
When I raise my hands toward Your
holy sanctuary.

Carry my voice on the wings of the
wind,
Let my plea turn Your head.
My palms outstretched implore You
now,
By Your hands I hope to be fed.

3 Do not drag me away with the wicked
And with those who practice injustice,
Who speak peace with their neighbors,
While evil is in their hearts.

Safely encircled in the night,
Sitting still, near by the fire,
Don't swat me, like some pestering swarm
Of hypocrites who conspire.

4 Give *back* to them according to their work and according to the evil of their practices;
Give *back* to them according to the work of their hands;
Repay them what is due them.

Squelch the hackers who stealthily steal,
Who burglarize in the night.
Turn the table on their tricks,
Set their disrupting all aright.

5 Because they do not regard the works of the LORD
Nor the deeds of His hands,
He will tear them down and not build them up.

Willow-brained fools walk from Your will,
And miss the feast You spread.
You decompose their rotting shows,
Then they fight You 'til they're dead.

6 Blessed be the LORD,
Because He has heard the sound of my pleading.

I stood to stretch my arms out wide,
Your compassion flowing came.
My heart then soared from thrill inside,
You lit love's lingering flame.

7 The LORD is my strength and my shield;
My heart trusts in Him, and I am helped;
Therefore my heart triumphs,
And with my song I shall thank Him.

You course the blood that fills my veins,
You shield me from abuse,
I fall secure in Your care again,
And You release my singing muse.

8 The LORD is their strength,
And He is a refuge of salvation to His anointed.

Ever stable, You still stand,
Steeled with restoring strength,
To bear the fears of all who call,
Born to love life's full length.

9 Save Your people and bless Your inheritance;
Be their shepherd also, and carry them forever.

Scoop up Your people once again,
Embrace them in Your fold,
Ever watching, always guarding,
On the trail toward Your safe stronghold.

Safe and secure in the Shepherd's arms, take some time to release what lingers in disquiet.

Taking Reflections with You

Beyond the sirens of life is a place of compassion that is safe in silent calm.

- How did this psalm touch on your insecurities with *particular words* that ignite your urge to cry for help?
- In the psalm, how did you see God as a "first responder" to the emergencies that have come up in your life? Did you see God as a Rock for you in any new way?
- How did this psalm get you in touch with your overwhelmed emotions? What did you discover about how security and emergencies impact *who you are*?
- What comfort did you discover in your *relationship with* God? Can you identify with being carried by the Great Shepherd, no matter what is happening around you?
- What did you experience of God as one who *speaks words of comfort* to you?
- What is your *cry for help* in your own words?

Final Embrace

Desperation is never expected. It is an unwelcome occurrence that demands a response to survive. Let the worry that wriggles in your head be acknowledged and then let your prayer be spoken and resolved.

Emergency.
Can't.
You.
See.
My life's a tragedy.
I need.
I plead.
I concede.
My fears impede.
Be.
My.
Rock.
Personified.
Made alive.
Rest, not strive.
Stability, not notoriety.
Security, not propriety.
Love's sensibility, not wild and crazy.
I've seen all that.
Living on the fat.
I'm done with that.
Never going back.
Listening.
Lifting.
Redirecting.
Refocusing.
Sanctuarying.
From.
The.
Cruel Crowd.
Speaking peace.
But.
Ripping.
To.
Pieces.
Those Hypocrites.
I seek a harbor.
Asylum forever.
Needing love's true arbor.
Heard.
Answered.
Blessed.
Shielded.
Yielded.
In Your love revealed.
Heart rejoicing.
Feet dancing, fast pacing.
Finding celebration's interlacing.
With the Shepherd finally interfacing.
In a People Party.
Save and protect.
For life's intersect.
Shalom's final project.
Embraced.
Sustained.
Forever.

Psalm 29

Seeing and Hearing Anew

Ascribe to the Lord *the glory due his name;*
worship the Lord *in the splendor of his holiness.*
(Psalm 29:2 NIV)

Surveying the Garden

Discovery is our growing edge. It makes us feel alive. It is a step beyond casual observation to a deeper understanding that connects us.

Our encounter with reality involves attuning our thinking with what already exists. We may call this curiosity, education, or scientific investigation. It is our extending frontier.

Think about your relationship to the sun. The sun has always been the center of our solar system. You were not born with this knowledge; recognizing this reality took time and insight as others opened your understanding.

As a child, understanding the skies was a mystery that required a learning process to comprehend their nature, movements, and many colors. Now you easily recognize the appearances of sunrise and sunset, as well as the changing relationship between the earth and the sun. Your mind became attuned to thinking from a new point of view. That change of mind is referred to as a paradigm shift.

Psalm 29 is a paradigm-shifting experience. This shift is the move from taking things for granted to seeing something anew in the world around us. We are invited to awaken to the personal presence of God who runs it all. He did not make it and leave; he still accompanies his creation.

With all its diverse activities, the whole garden of God's creation displays God's overseeing. The world is not a mistake nor was it made by chance; it has been developed uniquely, one step at a time.

A thunderstorm may compel us to say, "Wow!" But even more, when we see the beauty of the Creator at work, we might cry, "Glory!" We have glimpsed anew the reality of our world as magnificently woven together. We comprehend that it is sustained and still being created by God's personal involvement.

Our eyes, once veiled in darkness, now begin to see. Our ears, once closed, now hear the voice that calms all storms and speaks "peace" to our hearts.

"Peace to you," he says, with a smile that calms you to your toes. "This kind of peace I have for you is something you have never felt before. It is not the absence of strife but the overwhelming presence of My embrace. Let Me take your breath away, not from a squeeze, but from a deep satisfaction of being encompassed by My love."

Into the Garden with God

Seeing seems natural, like looking at a mountain or a person's body. But a complex story must be told to move beyond the seen to understand.

Hearing goes deeper, as we listen to those who have explored the landscape or the complexity of the body. Hearing is a deeper science that goes beyond the moment and the surface without dismissing the reality of what we see.

Knowing God requires seeing Jesus and hearing what he said about his Father. We need a paradigm shift to hear from Jesus's point of view. This opens the physical world for exploration.

Looking at Jesus is hard. He is not standing in front of us. The Bible helps us hear and explore based on what the writers saw and heard. This is a method of observation that allows for seeing and hearing to understand.

Many people do not want to listen to Jesus as God. They want to trim him down to just a human, reducing him to be just like us. But there is so much more.

This psalm reawakens our need to discover the Master of the Universe again. The wildness of the natural world responds to his call, and the world bespeaks his artistry and mastery.

God created the order that became the basis of science. Science studies the world as an orderly domain, exploring the beauty of its patterns, properties, and possibilities. Jesus made everything and cares for all. Therefore, faith and science are not separate; they are two perspectives for understanding.

This psalm awakens our eyes and ears so we may learn to see and hear as Jesus sees. We often think of the world as impersonal, a world of objects. When we do, we profoundly diminish our awareness of God's power and personal presence.

However, when viewed as a creation, it takes on a new character as God's handiwork, but most people miss this intentional, creative dimension.

Even Jesus's disciples struggled to comprehend Jesus's mastery over creation. In a storm on the lake, tossed in the boat, they fretted while he fell asleep. They had a hard time attuning to his sense of reality.

Jesus's disciples were not attuned to his full nature as God and human:

> **After dismissing the crowd, they took Him along with them in the boat, just as He was; and other boats were with Him. [37] And a fierce gale of wind developed, and the waves were breaking over the boat so much that the boat was already filling *with water.* [38] And *yet Jesus* Himself was in the stern, asleep on the cushion; and they woke Him and said to Him, "Teacher, do You not care that we are perishing?" [39] And He got up and rebuked the wind and said to the sea, "Hush, be still." And the wind died down and it became perfectly calm. [40] And He said to them, "Why are you afraid? Do you still have no faith?" [41] They became very much afraid and said to one another, "Who, then, is this, that even the wind and the sea obey Him?"**
>
> (Mark 4:36–41 NASB)

Our human capacity to recognize the extraordinary is limited. We are often overwhelmed by great art and miss the artist's wonder.

Once properly oriented to the divine artist, we may perceive his majesty. It is displayed in the dance of creation, all that lives a dynamic life at his bidding. The art is not the Artist. But the art is an expression of his overwhelming presence.

God desires to realign all creation to himself. So our whole being shouts out, "Glory!" when we encounter the kaleidoscopic wonder of God's self-giving. When two hearts truly meet, the heavens let loose a laugh of joy.

Get ready to take on the storm. Come now, as the wind dances, the clouds whisk by, and the thunderstorm puts on a display. Sit on the porch and enjoy the show. Jesus is waiting, waving to you to share an elegant rocking chair and throwing you a luxurious blanket.

Jesus says: "Watch and breathe in the wonder of my Father's delight. Hear Him shouting out his empowering voice that rumbles in the depths. Hear My Spirit's breath in the whistling wind, in a twirling dance with the trees. Let My wonder give you confidence that you are in the hands of a Mighty God. You are in the hands of grace—fully alive."

Get ready to enjoy the show.

Visions of Paradise

As we walk the path into the garden, we are surrounded by fields of air, electricity, water, and other interlaced systems that sustain us. You can't see all of them; you know they are there when you remember what you have been taught. The same will be true along today's path.

Along the Garden Path

On the Path of Life, God is both hidden and revealed.

In the opening glimpses of this psalm, we see what God has made, but we do not see God—the Artist is hidden.

As we hear voices calling out, we are open to recognizing the revealed splendor of God.

Words, especially names, connect us to the reality they refer to. When Adam and Eve named the animals in the garden, they became personally connected to them. Naming is endearing.

In this psalm, the heavenly hosts give words to discern God's attributes, to notice God's power and persistence. They reveal he is present to meet us and embrace our lives. As the storm mounts, we may hum the tune of "How Great Thou Art," considering all his hands have made.

We hear God's name echoing like thunder across the landscape. He speaks to all creation, even as it whispers his wonder. Without words, we hear the voices declaring God's glory and beckoning us to allegiance.

At the same time, he calls us to stand against all the false gods of this earth, silent idols who try to seduce human attention.

Real value is found only in the Living God. He is the source of our every breath and all the winds that herd the clouds around. Even where we cannot see him, we sense his presence and respond to his majesty as the Creator. The Psalms help us find words.

And the storm comes. The voice of God booms. You may not make out the words, but this is God's liberation language, just a part of giving the world space to grow and interrelate.

Miraculously, the light speaks, low and rumbling as it penetrates to the deepest parts of the earth with the heart of a Father who knows his children. This God at play impacts all.

Like the day of Pentecost, the winds of God's power rush through this place. The tongues of fire and flashing light filled the air with words unknown and yet wonderful.

The world is hearing and yet not fully comprehending what is happening. But all the world pays attention. All know that God is present and speaks a language their ears cannot comprehend, but their heart can hear.

Like celebrating priests, the human race embraces the moment, crying out, "Glory to God." This answering wave of wonder replies to the grace of God's self-giving.

The chaos has passed, and we are on a pilgrimage, sharing his presence and becoming more attached to him.

The King speaks a word of hope and gives us his kiss of peace. We are silent, having heard his voice in the tumult and serenity. His love is persistent.

Grab your seat and blanket and soak it all in, ready to breathe out a glorious, "Awesome!"

Indwelling the Garden

1 Ascribe to the LORD, sons of the
mighty,
Ascribe to the LORD glory and
strength.

2 Ascribe to the LORD the glory due
His name;
Worship the LORD in holy attire.

3 The voice of the LORD is on the
waters;
The God of glory thunders,
The LORD is over many waters.

4 The voice of the LORD is powerful,
The voice of the LORD is majestic.

5 The voice of the LORD breaks the
cedars;
Yes, the LORD breaks the cedars of
Lebanon in pieces.

6 He makes Lebanon skip like a calf,
And Sirion like a young wild ox.

Exclamations fill the air,
for Him who tender for us cares,
Joy befits His Name.
Emphasize His power wide,
which forms the air and
countryside,
Loving all He claims.

Elevate in every gate,
with tales of His feats of late,
Yes, name them, every one.
Celebrate the meal that heals,
Come eat with One whose beauty
reveals,
Unveiled as the sun.

Listen now His song is rising
The waves crash in reply,
Thunder punctuates His calling,
From afar, the Spirit flies.

Booming down to drown the sound,
Great falls now bow in awe.
His whisper bids the mountains rise,
Starting Spring's reblooming
thaw.

He splits the air and forests too,
His tongue divides the stand.
No barricade shall stay His way,
He clears with a sweep of His
hand.

The glaciered peaks all dance for joy,
Like ewes in frolicking fields,
And majestic mountains of the North
Laugh with His mirth revealed.

7 The voice of the LORD divides flames of fire.

Up the lights to flood the stage
Let timbrel sounds unfurl.
Let your sound-bursts clap to the heights,
And Your eyes blaze 'round the world.

8 The voice of the LORD shakes the wilderness;
The LORD shakes the wilderness of Kadesh.

The windy plain gets whirled round,
As You whistle from where You stand.
The dunes move molten, drifting on,
As You sculpt the sifting sand.

9 The voice of the LORD makes the deer give birth
And strips the forests bare;
And in His temple everything says, "Glory!

You press the woodland life, so still,
Through a winter, hard to bear.
But spring comes like a newborn fawn
And the world cries, "He is there!"

10 The LORD sat as King at the flood;
Yes, the LORD sits as King forever.

Enthroned above all earthly events
You wade right through the flood,
Forever crowned as the Sovereign One,
With the world as Your blooming rosebud.

11 The LORD will give strength to His people;
The LORD will bless His people with peace.

Surround and indwell us with Your Voice,
That we may fondly hear.
Cover us from all chaotic blare
And bring Your peace so near.

Taking Reflections with You

You can take off your rain gear now.

- What words in this psalm gave you visions or reflections on storms and how they make you feel about God? What images stick with you?

- What about God's voice and the glory of God made you want to discover more and see God in a new way?
- If God sees the thunderstorm as his beloved work, can you grasp that you are even more wondrously made? What did you discover about God's ultimate goal of bringing peace and presence to free you to be *who you are*?
- What does this psalm open for you in your *relationship with* God? Heavenly beings are announcing the glory of God, so you can get closer. What is opened for you to discover about the glory of God in your journey with him?
- What do you *hear God say to you* in the beauty and wonder of creation, as well as the storms and erosion?
- What *wordless ways can you respond* that echo back to His creation of all that surrounds you?

Final Embrace

A lightning flash in the night comes as a surprise and awakens all your senses. You are a recipient of energy unfurling and reenvisioning all that can be seen. We are transformed for a moment in encountering the mystery of what is powerful and penetrating—it could kill you or move you to awe. Such is the invitation of the words that follow, living in receptive marveling, not at a still small voice, but at the thunder that says, "I Am."

Pyrotechnics
Earth sonics.
        Voices
            Descending
                Like
                    Lightening.
                        Frightening
                              Or
                Enlightening?
          Flashing
              Dashing
                   Silence shattering.
                       Raindrops scattering.

Thunder scatting.
All overwhelming.
Glory.
Why all the worry?
Can grace, like snow, flurry?
Seas,
Oceans,
Lakes,
Rivers,
All in a hurry.
The truth is getting blurry.
I need Your voice with clarity.
Not just an act of charity.
The storm has gotten inside of me.
I need to see you mightily.
To bathe in Your endless majesty.
You win.
No match.
You batten the hatch.
Storm.
Squall.
Tornado tall.
You got it all.
Gale.
Hail.
Hurricane's tail.
You never fail.
You hold every kind of weather.
With me whenever.
Your glory.
That's forever.
Your peace.
Your life-giving rain.
For whomsoever.
Only You sustain.
Love's final endeavor.
Voice.
Spoken.

Psalm 30

Cycles of Renewal

For his anger lasts only a moment, but his favor lasts a lifetime;
weeping may stay for the night, but rejoicing comes in the morning.
(Psalm 30:5 NIV)

Surveying the Garden

Do aspects of your life need renewal?

What does it take for you to feel prepared for another day?

Maybe, for you, having enough healthy food feels like a luxury. Maybe having one good friend could make all the difference in feeling whole. Every human needs to be cared for, but for many, renewing patterns of life are missing.

Feeling whole should not be considered extravagant. Being whole includes our minds, emotions, bodies, and relationships. The life offered by God touches all this and more.

This psalm guides us through rhythms of renewal like a day in a spiritual spa, where we can launder our clothes. But only one person knows how to accomplish this kind of washing, inside and out—the Living God.

Don't you love that smell of fresh laundry and the warmth as it soothes your skin? That moment awakens the experience of renewal. Smell and touch begin to awaken a sense of well-being.

Jesus sends his Spirit to renew us daily, so we know who we are and soak in God's renewal of love for us. It may not come with smells and tactile joy, but our spirit is renewed with the freedom and peace to face another day.

Refreshing our body and soul can include a breath of fresh air that resets our mindset. The garden we have been exploring is one place of renewal.

In God's garden, the renewal of the relationship is the key; his presence is the context in which it will happen. His voice penetrates our hearts, and our bodies calm.

Awareness of what weighs us down is often absent—what needs to be cleaned, mended, or restored within us. We are often blind to our vulnerabilities and weaknesses. Survival is our focus.

Enduring life and avoiding death is too narrow a scope for our well-being. We often find ourselves stuck in emotional paralysis, which creates blind spots. We need a wash-and-rinse cycle.

The right person's insightful touch on our body and soul can find and fix troubled spots. This part of the garden is created for that exploration.

Lodged in the watchtower of our minds, we judge ourselves and others. Our narrow perception prevents us from acknowledging what is truly happening for us.

We protect the calm space inside by covering over invasive concerns. We disarm the alarm system so everyone will leave us alone. But this is one step away from death by detachment.

Today, embrace life's rich adventures with the One whose divine being makes each day new and fresh.

Turn down your anxieties and anticipations for a moment. Jesus is with you and sees the weight of worry. He wants to give you the weight of glory that lifts and renovates your waning life.

Let his eyes see right into you and melt the burdens that distract and defeat your joy. Silently, he motions you toward the garden with him. Feel the safe sensations that come with the release of tension and the rekindling of delight.

Into the Garden with God

The Bible is full of garden paths for renewal, and this is true of most of Jesus's stories.

But the backstory of Jesus's life and this psalm contain flashes of near-death and abuse as well as times of joy and celebration.

Jesus endured the pits by spending time with his Father. He leaned into his Father's future. He knew his journey was for the greater goal of human flourishing. His was the great act of the Healer who renews.

Jesus brought more than physical health to humanity. He brought relational health, the restoration of relationships that had fractured and developed distance and resistance.

The Apostle Paul lived through similar seasons and phases of weariness and renewal. He was a big-hearted caregiver, which meant he had a lot of exposure to abuse. But he did not allow the trauma of verbal and bodily harm to get to him. He encouraged the church in Corinth, saying:

> **For our momentary, light affliction is producing for us an eternal weight of glory far beyond all comparison.**
> (2 Corinthians 4:17)

Paul had the sensibilities to know what was temporary and would pass. He knew the Spirit was ever active in taking broken situations, finding ways to bind them up, and helping those in need.

Glory is coming. This implies the very presence of God in all his grandeur. All God's love, power, presence, grace, and holiness saturate restoration spaces. His glory wakes us up to our pain and causes the healing of wounds to bring hope.

Glory creates joy, which comes from meeting the Artist and Healer. He is making all things new and restoring the old; he will do this, not once, not twice, but every time we need the Spirit's spa to start afresh.

Today's walk will require stripping off old emotions and expectations, washing away the stains of shame, blame, and guilt.

A truly restorative state is the result of allowing a soothing massage to remove the tensions that come from the pursuit of grandeur. We have no idea how the temptation to strive can hinder us. We think we should be in control of our lives. This is a myth. Release, receive the gift of grace, and let the Spirit address the burdens, disappointment, and ingratitude. The gift of renewal comes from authentic personal connections.

Allow yourself to be pampered and loved despite yourself. Afterwards, you will need to be re-dressed in celebratory clothes. We are clothed as new persons in Christ and renewed to echo his life.

Welcome to the Spa of the Spirit. Nothing is left untouched here. Shake off any resistance and yield to the One called the Paraclete, meaning "One called alongside to help." Relax and receive the healing touch.

Visions of Paradise

Breathe deeply and open your inner world to be bathed with hope. Consider a bit of celebratory dancing as you proceed down the path.

Along the Garden Path

You may think of a spa as a place of luxury, but in this case, it refers to a place for healing, restorative waters, and touch. It is a place where body, mind, and soul are restored in the hands of a skilled practitioner.

We are not always aware that we need a caring touch. Today, we discover that nurturing is not extravagant. Self-care is not selfish. There is a divine urge to bring the sick to wellness, the downtrodden to be encouraged, and the outcast to find hospitable treatment. Today, this is for you.

This psalm's path of healing addresses the human poles of emotion. Most people have drama in their lives that may include grief, loneliness, anxiety, pain and aches, or the fear of death. They all build callouses around the heart.

Our path leads to a place where we find ourselves energized, content, connected, grateful, joyfully resilient. Our renewal means feeling focused and prepared for meeting challenges and establishing healthy connections.

Psalm 30 begins by recognizing that we are lifted up by God's hand. We lift our eyes and attention toward the One who is the source of our status as healed people.

We must do this if we ever hope to truly heal. Health is not a built-in capability. It needs support. To truly embrace the possibilities of a spiritually abundant life, a breakthrough is needed.

Now, because God loves us, he occasionally gets jealous and angry. That is love's protective face. When we engage in self-destructive, abusive behaviors, his displeasure serves as a momentary warning and calls us back to safety. That response is like a mother shouting from the porch to children about to hurt themselves or each other.

God is intent on bringing us back to his secure fondness, and away from our neurotic insecurities. He wants us to enjoy favor at his table.

This psalm reminds us that the grief that accompanies us as we fall asleep after a tough day will not last forever. Like an obnoxious and unwelcome guest, it will leave when the first light of morning breaks through the shadows.

When we awaken to the light and peace of God's loving presence, we are filled with a soothing sense of jubilation. With the dawn, we welcome the One who awakens us to his reality. He opens our eyes beyond our shortsighted frustrations and disappointments.

Sometimes, our concerns are buried. We think we can figure life out all by ourselves. We naively think all is well, we are in control, and nothing could go wrong. But feeling secure in our capabilities is its own affliction.

With our blind certainty, we cannot see how much we are missing. We are captivated by our desires. We want the "good life" that the world promises, and we think we can attain it. However, a meaningful life has little to do with being self-made; it is about experiencing life as a gift and being thankful for all that is provided. Actual contentment and confidence are the gift of God.

In the end, Jesus's love is tougher than our ignorance. His goal includes healing our lives as a whole, creating a healthy person in mind and body, able to make secure connections with others. He has opened a way for cleansing.

As you walk out from your spa treatment, feeling rejuvenated, your heart might fill with a song of content, impossible to be silenced. This ought not to last for only a moment. This gift stretches into forever.

Shake off whatever holds you back and enter. . . .

Indwelling the Garden

1 I will exalt You, LORD, for You have lifted me up,
And have not let my enemies rejoice over me.

The hush of awe shall fill me up,
Then I shall bursting tell,
Once again, You found me lost,
Reclaimed my life to health.

2 LORD my God, I cried to You for help, and You healed me.

Healer of all woeful souls,
Answering my life's pain,
You alone have been my help
Through loss, You bring me gain.

3 LORD, You have brought up my soul from Sheol;
You have kept me alive, that I would not go down to the pit.

Resurrect from the verge of death,
Extend unfailing hands;
Your reviving breath will fill my lungs,
Your gift to help me stand.

4 Sing praise to the LORD, you His godly ones,
And praise the mention of His holiness.

Exhaling now, we voice Your praise,
"Come all, let music flow."
A well of thanks within us grows,
As Your Spirit's joy now blows.

5 For His anger is but for a moment,
His favor is for a lifetime;
Weeping may last for the night,
But a shout of joy comes in the morning.

Displeasure, like a laser light,
Intends a healing touch.
Pleasure shines in the waking sun,
Our little restored to much.

6 Now as for me, I said in my
prosperity,
"I will never be moved."

Naive, in my days of plenty,
I thought my roots were deep,
Distracted from Your goodness,
My life was a famished heap.

7 LORD, by Your favor You have made
my mountain to stand strong;
You hid Your face, I was dismayed.

I felt as secure as a mountain range,
Against the scourge of time,
But when I lost my sense of You,
Out of touch, I struggled to
climb.

8 To You, LORD, I called;
And to the Lord I pleaded for
compassion:

Awakened in the darkness still,
To You, my plea was turned,
Yielding my will, so my needs might be
filled,
Praying I had not been spurned.

9 "What gain is there in my blood, if I
go down to the pit?
Will the dust praise You? Will it
declare Your faithfulness?

Spare me now from this draining
dread,
With my life spilled on the ground.
What value comes from the earth
stained red?
While I'm alive, my heart resounds.

10 Hear, LORD, and be gracious to me;
Lord, be my helper."

Listen gently, calm my cry,
Give comfort as You come.
Mend me, sitting by my bed,
Touch deep where my pain comes
from.

11 You have turned my mourning into
dancing for me;
You have untied my sackcloth and
encircled me with joy,

Now, my weeping turns to waltzing,
The dusk has turned to dawn,
Ashes have turned to fine apparel;
My sadness has birthed a song.

12 That my soul may sing praise to You
and not be silent.
LORD my God, I will give thanks to
You forever.

Yesterday's tone was so reserved,
Now I tweet a merry tune,
Master of Joy, You alone will I
serve,
Forever, from gratefulness hewn.

Taking Reflections with You

- What *words or phrases* brought images to mind that gave you a sense of your journey from brokenness to wholeness?
- Did you see God in a new way, as the Master of the Spa, touching your body and spirit? Where were the tender places?
- How did this psalm create a desire for regular renewal? What did you discover about *who you are* when you are being renewed that gives you hope for being made new?
- How does this psalm awaken a healing possibility in your *relationship with* God? Can you see that the hard and good times may be used to grow you to be all you can be by building a healthy, intimate life with him?
- What can you imagine *Jesus saying to you* as you lie on a table and he is rubbing the oil of gladness on your back? Is he asking questions or telling you something to soothe your soul?
- As you sit in a steaming public bath, with nowhere to go, Jesus by your side, what do *you want to say* to end your spa day to feel clean inside and out?

Final Embrace

The scent of lavender brings a sense of serenity, calm, and grace. The color purple is often associated with royalty and refinement. Smell this bouquet as a reminder of the rhythms of renewal. Let your senses speak to you. Take this at spa speed, which is slow and relaxing, allowing you to soak in the sensations of restoration. Try one second between each line.

Daddy, lift me up.
Hold me.
Heal me.
I need.
You.
Only You.
Will do.
To be renewed.

Glancing down.
I see a pit.
A grave not lit.
Death's final spit.
Life's fabric ripped.
Surround me.
With a circle of friends.
Our hearts to mend.

Singing.
Without end.
Your Name.
Ascends.
Holy remembrance.
A flash.
Of wrath.
Then fountains flow.
A healing bath.
A restoring path.
Love's aftermath.
Drip of tears.
In the dead of night.
Turns to floods of joy.
In daybreak's light.
Cleansing me.
From foolish times.
Naive.
Arrogantly blind.
An overconfident bind.
Sightless.
Witless.
How did I miss it?
I thought that I was mountain strong.
Pride's erosion showed I was wrong.
Without vision.
Lost my way.
A doleful cry.
Was all I could pray.
I thought that You thought.
I had gone astray.
Like wine poured out.
I was wasting away.
Return to me.
This dirge relieve.
The wailing.
Sighing.
Mourning Song.
Ignite my feet.
To whirl complete.
Mourner's clothes destroy.
Release my joy.
Finest attire employ.
Somersaulting like a tumbling boy.
Living out love's greatest ploy.
A life of thanks to enjoy.
No more silence.
No more fear.
No looking how it might appear.
I'll burst with singing.
I'll laugh out loud.
I'll praise you daily.
Dancing outside.
But my heart is bowed.
Renovated.
Renewed.
Resolved.
Rested.
In You.

Afterword

We are on our adventure through the garden of the Psalms together with the Living God!

This book began between 1998 and 1999 at Regent College, Vancouver, BC, Canada, as I engaged in a postdoctoral program in that lovely city. Cam and Kay MacIntosh hosted me in that city, and much of the poetry was written in their home.

Gary Deddo, then at InterVarsity Press, encouraged me to expand the vision, making it a more comprehensive project. James Baker, from Adelaide, Australia, helped me wrestle to find the garden theme that brought it all together. These have been encouragers for whom I have deep gratitude.

My wife, Cindy, has been my patron saint, making space for me to write, read, and edit, capturing and clarifying the beauty in fine-tuning. This project would not have been possible without her.

I have readers who provide me with honest feedback, constructive criticism, and unwavering support. Jeff and Tanya Huber, Marko and Shelley Jukanovich, Jimmy and Linda Grierson, Becky Brown, and Jonathan Parisot head the list of these informative eyes.

Bono and U2 became an inspiration to me as I taught a graduate course, "U2 and Theological Mission," at Northwest University in 2015. I love how deeply they reflect the Bible, especially the Psalms, and bring it to life in today's world. I warm my hands and heart at the fire they ignite in the world.

My daughter, Abigail, has once again added a dimension of artistic engagement that opens the door to enter the work and participate in life together. She is a gift!

My deepest gratitude to Anna Lyn Horky, who has done superb editing on my Face to Face trilogy and my Karl Barth's Church Dogmatics for Everyone series. She is thorough and sees each project through to a beautiful end.

Jeremy Begbie is a hero of mine, bringing a world of artistic insight to engage theology, Scripture, and the glory of God in the church and world. His words in the foreword are gold to me.

Carl Bromley has been a Godsend as an editor. He saw the value in this series and has been a wonderful advocate in a world of competitive publishing. I am honored to work with him and his team.

This book is the first of five volumes created to spend time in the Garden of God, which we call the Psalms. I pray you may indwell these pages and those to come, not only hearing the words, but through them hearing the Voice of the One to whom they invite us.

Joyfully in Christ,
Marty Folsom

Works Considered

Alter, Robert. *The Book of Psalms: A Translation with Commentary*. W. W. Norton & Company, 2007.

Anderson, Fred R. *Singing God's Psalms: Metrical Psalms and Reflections for Each Sunday in the Church Year*. Eerdmans Publishing Co., 2016.

Bonhoeffer, Dietrich. *Psalms: The Prayer Book of the Bible*. Fortress Press, 1974.

Brown, William P. *Seeing the Psalms: A Theology of Metaphor*. WJK, 2002.

Brueggemann, Walter. *From Whom No Secrets are Hid: Introducing the Psalms*. WJK, 2014.

Brueggemann, Walter. *Israel's Praise: Doxology Against Idolatry and Ideology*. Fortress Press, 1988.

Brueggemann, Walter. *Praying the Psalms: Engaging Scripture and the Life of the Spirit*. Wipf and Stock, 2007.

Brueggemann, Walter, and William H. Bellinger Jr. *Psalms*. New Cambridge Bible Commentary. Cambridge University Press, 2014.

Brueggemann, Walter. *Spirituality of the Psalms*. Fortress Press, 2001.

Brueggemann, Walter. *The Psalms & the Life of Faith*. Edited by Patrick D. Miller. Fortress Press, 1995.

Craigie, Peter C., and Marvin E. Tate. *Psalms 1–50*. Vol. 19, 2nd ed. Word Biblical Commentary. Zondervan, 2004.

Davie, Donald, ed. *The Psalms in English*. Penguin, 1996.

Einstein, Albert, Sir James Jeans, and Theodore Dreiser et al. *Living Philosophies*. Simon and Schuster, 1931.

Freemantle, James S. *The Psalms of David*. HarperCollins, 2004.

Goldingay, John. *Psalms, Volume 1: Psalms 1–41*. Baker Commentary on the Old Testament. Baker, 2006.

Guite, Malcolm. *David's Crown: Sounding the Psalms*. Canterbury Press, 2021.

Guite, Malcolm. Malcolm Guite homepage. Accessed September 30, 2025. https://malcolmguite.wordpress.com/tag/psalms/.

Hopkins, Denise Dombkowski, and Michael S. Koppel. *Grounded in the Living Word: The Old Testament and Pastoral Care Practices*. Eerdmans, 2010.

Jensen, Irving L. *Psalms: A Self-Study Guide*. Moody Publishers, 1968.

Keller, Timothy. *The Songs of Jesus: A Year of Daily Devotions in the Psalms*. Penguin Random House, 2017.

Kidner, Derek. *Psalms 1–72: An Introduction & Commentary*. Tyndale Old Testament Commentaries. IVP, 1973.

Kohlenberger, John R., III. *The NIV Interlinear Hebrew-English Old Testament: Volume 3, Chronicles—Song of Songs*. Zondervan, 1982.

LeFebvre, Michael. *Singing the Songs of Jesus: Revisiting the Psalms*. Christian Focus, 2011.

The Learning Bible: Contemporary English Version. American Bible Society, 2000.

Lewis, C. S. *Reflections on the Psalms*. HarperCollins, 1961.

The Living Bible. Tyndale House Publishers, 1971.

Luther, Martin, quoted in Witvliet, John D., *The Biblical Psalms in Christian Worship: A Brief Introduction and Guide to Resources*. Eerdmans, 2007.

Mays, James L. *Psalms: Interpretation: A Bible Commentary for Teaching and Preaching*. John Knox Press, 1994.

Miller, Patrick D. *Interpreting the Psalms*. Fortress Press, 1986.

Miller, Patrick D. *They Cried to the Lord: The Form and Theology of Biblical Prayer*. Fortress Press, 1994.

Mowinckel, Sigmund. *The Psalms in Israel's Worship*. Eerdmans, 2004.

The New Jerusalem Bible: Reader's Edition. Doubleday, 1990.

Peterson, Eugene H. *Answering God: The Psalms as Tools for Prayer*. HarperCollins, 1989.

Peterson, Eugene H. *The Message: New Testament with Psalms and Proverbs in Contemporary Language*. NavPress, 1995.

Rhodes, Arnold B. *The Layman's Bible Commentary: The Book of Psalms*. Vol. 9. John Knox Press, 1978.

Robertson, O. Palmer. *The Flow of the Psalms: Discovering Their Structure and Theology*. P & R Publishing, 2015.

Schmutzer, Andrew J., and David M. Howard Jr. *The Psalms: Language for All Seasons of the Soul*. Moody Publishers, 2013.

Seif, Jeffrey L., Glenn D. Blank, and Paul Wilbur. *TLV Psalms with Commentary: Hope and Healing in the Hebrew Scriptures*. Destiny Image Messianic, 2012.

Shippey, Tom. *J.R.R. Tolkien: Author of the Century*. Houghton Mifflin, 2001.

Swenson, Kristin M. *Living Through Pain: Psalms and the Search for Wholeness*. Baylor University Press, 2005.

Tel, Martin, Joyce Borger, and John D. Witvliet, eds. *Psalms for All Seasons: A Complete Psalter for Worship*. Faith Alive Christian Resources, 2011.

Thornes, Tobias. *The Psalter in Rhyming Verse*. Wash House Publishing, 2021.

Waltke, Bruce K., and James M. Houston, with Erika Moore. *The Psalms as Christian Worship: A Historical Commentary*. Eerdmans, 2010.

Wieder, Laurance, ed. *The Poets' Book of Psalms: The Complete Psalter as Rendered by Twenty-Five Poets from the Sixteenth to the Twentieth Centuries*. Harper San Francisco, 1995.

Wieder, Laurance. *Words to God's Music: A New Book of Psalms*. Highland Books, 2003.

Wilson, Gerald H. *The NIV Application Commentary: Psalms Volume 1*. Zondervan, 2002.

Witvliet, John D. *The Biblical Psalms in Christian Worship: A Brief Introduction and Guide to Resources*. Eerdmans, 2007.